A great deal of time must be taken to build a true marriage .... A deep encounter rarely takes place in a few moments. It must be prepared for by hours of careful drawing together.

— Dr. Paul Tournier
(To Understand Each Other)

Secrets of a GROWING MARRIAGE

Building Our Commitment of Love

Roger and Donna Vann

Here's Life Publishers

San Bernardino, California 92402

SECRETS OF A GROWING MARRIAGE
Building Our Commitment of Love
by Roger and Donna Vann

Published by

 Here's Life Publishers

795 South Allen Street
P.O. Box 1576
San Bernardino, California 92402
ISBN 0-89840-080-5
Library of Congress Catalog Card 84-072940
HLP Product Number 950907

Unless otherwise indicated, Scripture quotations are from *The Holy Bible, New International Version,* © 1978 by New York International Bible Society, published by The Zondervan Corporation, Grand Rapids, Michigan, and used by permission. Other Scripture quotations are from *The Living Bible* (LB), © 1971 by Tyndale House Publishers, Wheaton, Illinois, and used by permission, and the New American Standard Bible (NAS), © The Lockman Foundation 1960, 1962, 1963, 1968, 1971, 1972, 1973, 1975, and are used by permission.

with love to our "young olive plants" —

Lisa, David and Millay

— and appreciation for their patience during
the writing of this book

Table of Contents

Acknowledgments

Before You Go

On Location

Back to Reality

Acknowledgments

For encouragement and editorial comment we are grateful to Joe and Diane Webb, Roger Randall, Linda Anderson, Jim Morud and Les Stobbe.

For faithfully serving through many hours of typing and/or babysitting, we deeply appreciate Tuija Tuomenen, Lynn Van Pykeren and especially Sieglinde Becker.

For their part in helping us get a feel for what Christian couples are experiencing, we give heartfelt thanks to the dozens of couples who filled out surveys or took field-test getaway weekends.

The Authors

Roger and Donna Vann bring a unique combination of education, work with young couples, and personal experience in marriage to this book on *Secrets of a Growing Marriage*. A graduate of the University of Texas, Roger is currently administrator of Here's Life Europe, after serving in both the campus and Here's Life America ministries in the United States. Donna, a graduate of Southwestern University in Texas, has worked in a bookstore, served as English teacher and as a freelance writer. The authors have three children, Lisa, a mid-teen, and David and Millay, both preschoolers. This book grew out of personally experiencing the benefits of regular retreats to improve communication in their marriage despite a hectic schedule of ministry.

Before You Go

Chapter 1
Your Marriage Garden

Even in the best of relationships, there are times when everything falls apart.

Like the day I simply answered with an honest "No!" Immediately I was pelted with a pair of shoes, three chunky travelogues, and assorted maps and papers.

My wife Donna had asked me a direct question about a certain aspect of our relationship. Foolhardily, I gave a blunt answer. That's when she bombarded me.

We decided we'd better take a walk and clear our thoughts. It took several hours of walking and talking over a two-day period before we could get our arms around the problem. Eventually, Donna began to grasp why I felt the way I did. And I began to see my own role in creating the rift.

It is frustrating when some hidden resentment pops to the surface in a marriage partnership, and there's no chance to talk. Like when your husband announces at breakfast that he won't be home for supper, and you greet it with a silence so thick he could spread it on his toast. Or when your wife slips her Mastercard bill under the stack of mail and leaves for the supermarket to avoid an explosion.

Wasn't it lucky that *we* just happened to have several hours free right when our big blow-up came?

"Luck" had nothing to do with it. This "free time" was carefully planned as part of our twice-yearly marriage retreat, a weekend when we get away together to seek growth as a couple.

Of course, our schedule did not include Donna's hitting me over the head with shoes. Nor did we set out to be quite so painfully open with each other.

But it happened, and we had the time to discuss from every

angle the issue that was dividing us. By Sunday night, we understood each other much better. Yet these insights, though gained through tears, did not drive us apart. We felt closer than ever before.

That same weekend I said to Donna, "This has been such a valuable time—I wish all of our married friends could take such a retreat." This book is the result.

Your Marriage Gardening Guide

Planning

A marriage relationship is like a garden. It must be plowed, fertilized, planted, watered and weeded. Donna and I want to plant in you the idea of taking a marriage retreat yourselves; we want to guide you in cultivating communication while you're on such a retreat; and we want to give you ideas on how to root your weekend experience into the soil of your daily lives.

We want you to have the joy, as we have, of watching new life and order spring up where once lay a tangled confusion of rocks and weeds. We've designed this volume, not as a marriage text, but as a handbook to be used again and again. Look upon it as your marriage gardening guide!

This "guide" is divided into three sections. The first, chapters 1 through 4, should be read prior to getting away for a retreat. This is important, as it will help develop the proper attitudes, as well as give you ideas on where and how to take a getaway.

The second section, chapters 5 through 13, is the retreat "workbook." Chapter 5 should be read as the retreat begins; it outlines the use of this section and of your Talkbook. Chapters 6 through 13 each cover one topic related to marriage, in a format that promotes discussion, mutual affirmation, prayer and taking action together.

The third section is designed to help you follow through on ideas generated on the retreat. How will these ideas make a difference in your daily lives? How can you continue to communicate constructively? See chapter 14. The third section also contains a bibliography of helpful publications, organized by subject, to be used before, during or after your retreat, or at any time!

I should explain that Donna is an equal partner in writing this volume. She did most of the actual writing, after long hours of ideas being tossed back and forth between us. For the sake of simplicity, however, "I" will refer to Roger throughout.

We realize that a weekend such as we propose is not a panacea for all marital ills. But for average Christian couples like Donna and me, who want to grow closer, the regular marriage retreat can be like marital fertilizer: It catalyzes growth.

Not yet convinced? Read on!

Planning

Chapter 2

It Takes Two to Grow

I recently experienced one of "life's most embarrassing moments." It happened, between appointments with businessmen, as I was filling my car's gas tank at a self-service station.

Now, for me pumping gas is an automatic reflex. Unhook nozzle, twirl "on" handle, insert nozzle in car, pump gas, replace nozzle on pump, pay, drive away. I could do it blindfolded.

Except on that particular day. I was in a hurry, my thoughts were elsewhere, and I unwittingly omitted one vital step.

As I gunned the gas to drive away, suddenly I felt as if a giant had reached down and grabbed my rear bumper with one hairy paw. Simultaneously, I heard an ear-splitting crash as glass and metal struck solid concrete.

I braked and leaped out to see the gas pump hose now painfully stretched to an unnatural twenty-foot length, with the nozzle still faithfully clinging to the opening of my gas tank. On the pavement lay the broken remains of the large metal-and-glass pump in a growing lake of gasoline.

Dazed, I asked, "What happened?"

Coasting on Automatic Pilot

That illustrates the situation in which many couples today find themselves. They've drifted along for quite a while with their relationship on "automatic pilot." Because everything seems fine and dandy, they are soothed into complacency. They figure, "Nothing's wrong with our marriage. Sure nice that we don't have to worry about a breakup, like so many other couples." Then, often quite suddenly, WHAM-SMASH. The whole structure crashes to the pavement before their disbelieving eyes.

A close friend of ours once bragged, "I may have some problems in life, but my marriage certainly isn't one of them. That's the one thing I can be sure of — we'll never have to worry about landing in the divorce court." Yet only a few short years later, she sat weeping over a divorce decree.

The Downward Drift

Building

At the gas station, I had mentally coasted on "automatic" when I should have paid more attention to the pump and nozzle. They were simple, everyday things, but capable of causing disaster if not operated properly. Similarly, a marriage left to run on the grooves of habit tends to drift downward. It can become locked in a deadly progression that is difficult to break, in spite of the partners' very good intentions. Emotional wreckage is the almost certain result.

The marriage progresses through three stages:

   I. - *Romance*
  II. - *Reality*
 III. - *Resignation/Reconstruction*

Stage I - ROMANCE

When two Christian partners come together to start their marriage garden, they are full of strong, positive feelings. They totally accept each other and continually feel surrounded by a warm glow.

Stage II - REALITY

Then the glow subsides, enabling each to see the mate's faults with disturbing clarity. They step back to take a more critical look and find that their spouse's weaknesses are springing up to form a barrier between them. At this stage they may futilely attempt to remake their partner into the "ideal mate" they'd like to have.

Stage III - RESIGNATION

The wall grows higher as more weaknesses and problems surface, until it raises a dividing barrier right down the middle of the garden! Feelings of coolness harden into resentment. Because the partners give up, they in effect establish separate lives. They may begin to seek other sources of fulfillment.

At this point, something far more dangerous than mere stagnation occurs. The hungry enemies of the marriage garden start crawling nearer, looking for ways to steal the fruit. They won't have difficulty, since the partners are divided, leaving each exposed and vulnerable to any attack. (We'll identify these slithering enemies in section II, chapter 7, which deals with spiritual oneness.)

Marriages need not end with mere resignation, though. God has a better plan called ...

Stage III - RECONSTRUCTION

Instead of letting problems build up into a barrier between them, partners can view each conflict, or block, as a joint project. Together, they can work to move the blocks from between them to the outer edge of the garden.

After a time, the very blocks that once separated them will become a unifying wall of defense around their garden. With the garden secure against enemy attack, the couple can concentrate on cooperative cultivation, and the marriage garden will flourish.

How can a couple break the downward drift cycle and produce a fruitful relationship? The partners need to work *as a twosome* to cultivate their marriage and to move the blocks. I believe that when one partner does all the work, God honors that person's faithfulness, but that is not His original design. God desires for both partners to labor together to bring about growth. Then the marriage patch will be filled with such large, healthy crops that it will attract the attention of even casual passersby.

One way to encourage this joint cultivation is to go on regular "dates" together. Donna and I go out for an evening about twice a month. We try not to make these merely passive escapes from the kids (although even that has tremendous value, especially for a wife) but to make them active times of interaction and planning.

Taking Time to Dig Deeper

Building

Genuine communication, however, requires quite a bit of time. It takes more than a couple of hours away from the house to uncover deeper issues. Even if a crucial topic does crop up over coffee, there's no time to deal with it. You pay the waitress and return home to the stresses that caused it in the first place.

Earlier I mentioned an incident in which Donna flung shoes and books at me. This prompted a discussion that was terribly necessary for the growth of our marriage. We repeatedly had swept something under the rug, and it was beginning to decay. Oh, we'd tried to deal with it for months in some pretty heavy late-night conversations. Since we usually were quite tired, the recurring pattern was that Donna would burst into tears and I would insist (sensibly, I thought), "Let's go to bed. We'll deal with this another time, when you're not so exhausted."

But it never happened. Like you, we have the noblest of intentions about relating to each other in more than a superficial way. It's just that kids and work and travel schedules and unexpected company and telephones and evening commitments won't let us. They all seem to unite in a conspiracy to prevent us from deep contact with each other.

So we never managed to get our feelings fully out in the open, where we could examine them at length impartially. That is, not until we retired from the world for a few days. Even then, we didn't start out in an unbiased mood — far from it! But as we talked and prayed together, gradually we both gained a healthy objectivity, which is next to impossible in the familiar setting of home.

We even telephoned our babysitter mid-retreat and asked if we could stay another day! She agreed, and we did. Our marriage hasn't been the same since.

As you can see, these weekends are more than second honeymoons (which also are valuable). They are opportunities for quality interaction. They provide time not only for curative conversation, but also for preventative, in the form of planning ahead. These retreats can help your family, even as it is being whirled around in society's centrifuge, come out unified, whole and growing closer with each passing year.

Ripe for a Getaway

Consider the following scene in the life of an average Christian couple.

John accelerated his car onto the freeway, joining the sluggish mass of the suburb-bound. He drove mechanically, his mind fixed on the big project brewing at the firm. *Work just seems to go from one deadline to another; I can't remember when there's ever been a letup.*

"Hi, hon," he called, stepping into the kitchen from the garage. Laurie muttered a greeting and continued to frown at the steaming pot of stew she was stirring, as if daring it to burn. She smiled at him fleetingly as his lips grazed her perspiring cheek.

John sighed. *What a welcome. I wish she'd leap into my arms the way she used to when I came home.* The kids chattered and squabbled over dinner in their usual fashion. Preoccupied as he was, John couldn't help sensing that Laurie was unusually quiet. *There's something on her mind — I've been getting signals of disappointment from her for the past few days. Well, she can't expect me to deal with it on a Monday night. I'm wrung out, and nothing ever stands in the way of Monday Night T.V. football. She knows that! Tuesday night will be soon enough.*

After John switched off the television set late that evening, he headed straight for bed. Laurie came around and sat down on his side. "John . . ." she began tentatively.

"Hon, let's just have prayer and lights out tonight," he cut in. "I'm dead tired. Will it keep till tomorrow?"

Laurie stiffened. *We never talk, really talk anymore. He's so preoccupied with his precious work! If he had any sensitivity for my feelings, he'd know what's bothering me.* But she merely said dully, "Did you forget, Mother's coming tomorrow?"

"Oh, yeah." John was too tired to digest the emotions that hit him following that statement. "I did forget, Hon. I'm sorry. But I'm really beat tonight." He held her hand and said a brief prayer before kissing her goodnight.

If he thinks he can gloss over this by being spiritual, he can think again! Laurie did not pray.

Building

Situations like this are not unusual. In fact, similar scenes have been played from time to time in my own marriage. I'd say John and Laurie are ripe for a getaway.

Admittedly it's not easy to coordinate such a time, totally away, without kids (see chapter 4 for ideas). But it's worth every ounce of effort. Compare it to making wise financial investments now, which will pay large dividends in the years to come.

Not Just Sweet Nothings

What will you talk about, once you've secluded yourselves from the world and are sitting face-to-face, with several hours stretching before you? "Sweet nothings" are great — for dessert. But most couples need to grapple with some specific issues, to get down to the real "meat" of what it means to live in a Christ-honoring union. Therefore, we've provided an abundance of questions, organized by topics to help you talk about the deeper needs of your marriage and family.

Before determining which issues to address, we surveyed about fifty Christian couples. They deemed the following areas of concern essential for such a workbook:

Communication
Spiritual oneness
Understanding each other
Sexual intimacy
Living according to priorities
Finances
Childraising
Reaching out to others

While the list could be longer, these are the major blocks that either divide or unite and protect a Christian marriage. You will find a chapter on each of these topics in section II. These chapters are designed to guide a couple as they take hold of each block and move it from the barrier to a unifying garden wall.

Donna and I have worked hard to make this marriage retreat workbook realistic for average Christian couples like ourselves. Even if you can't swing a whole weekend, don't give up! We offer other alternatives in chapter 4.

My wife and I hope to be married for at least fifty more years. We have no intention of that being represented by fifty calendars on the wall, but rather by an ever-growing garden, well-kept and flourishing, a delight to all who see it. And we are willing to invest the time and energy necessary to produce such a relationship.

In What Stage Is <u>Your</u> Marriage?

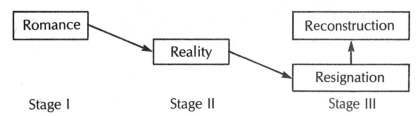

Stage I   Stage II   Stage III

After all, a marriage relationship deserves no less attention than a businessman would give a project at his office, than a preacher would devote to his weekly sermon, or than a student would use to prepare for an upcoming exam. Saying "I didn't have time to study," is a laughably lame excuse. So is saying, "We didn't have time to work on our marriage." Just as study and learning go together, so do purposeful communication and a healthy marriage. Even the Lord Jesus, though He was not married, took special times away with those closest to Him.

I get excited when I think of all the ways my own marriage will be tilled and nourished by our regular, planned escapes. The same benefits are available for you — just keep reading!

Chapter 3
Test Your Marriage Soil

As the two of you set out to cultivate your marriage garden, you'll first want to examine the soil. Bend down and scoop up a little in your hands. Is it full of pebbles? Is it too sandy? Does it contain enough minerals and nutrients to sustain life?

Just as inadequate soil will produce a scraggly garden, so a deficiency in certain essential relationship nutrients will result in a scraggly marriage. A couple might get away several times each year, but those efforts will be wasted if the basic elements are missing.

As you test the soil of your marriage, I hope you will find three essential ingredients. Each directly relates to your ability to receive and give God's love. The three nutrients are:

GRACE
COMMITMENT
THE HOLY SPIRIT

FIRST NUTRIENT: GRACE

The first essential ingredient is grace. That may sound a bit holier-than-thou, so let's crack it open and see what is inside. Our thesaurus lists under grace: *charity, lenience, mercy, clemency, forgiveness.*

In other words, grace means relating to someone in a forgiving way. The other person may be totally undeserving of forgiveness, but grace says I choose to forgive and love anyway.

Let me illustrate. I have a bad habit of "not having time for" certain household projects, just before I leave on a trip. Many times I have promised to clean out the basement or garage, but

I got in a hurry and put it off again. I am glad that my wife usually doesn't add this to a running mental list of "Roger's typical failures." Instead, she says something like, "Can we put this on your calendar for the Saturday after you get back?" That's grace.

Also at times I've started to pack for a business trip and discovered that my favorite shirt wasn't ironed. I could easily attack Donna, saying, "That shirt's been in the ironing basket for three weeks! What do you do all day, anyway?" Well, even I can see that with three kids, my wife does have a few other things to do. I make a mental note to call the shirt to her attention a few days ahead of my next trip. Then if she's too busy at that moment, I go and iron the shirt myself. But I don't act like Marvin Martyr, implying that she failed as a homemaker.

The Performance Pitfall

Relating in grace has an opposite, called the "performance standard." The performance standard demands, "Do this, do that, and then you will be acceptable to me. Then, and only then, will I love you." I recently saw an extreme example of this in Ann Lander's column. A woman wrote to say that her husband actually had a little black book in which he kept a written record — with ratings — of their love-making. That guy obviously never had heard of grace!

As I write, I'm also reminded of a vibrant Christian couple we know, who are having an impact for the Lord on the lives of many others. A few years ago, the wife had the courage to respond in grace to the painful fact of her husband's unfaithfulness. She probably felt like saying, "You lowdown two-timer! If you ever see her again, I'll have you tarred and feathered! You'd better change your ways if you ever hope to receive any more affection from me." But she didn't. Grace means saying, "I hate what you did, but I still love *you*."

Most of us, I hope, won't have to learn the meaning of grace on such a massive scale. Yet sometimes the little irritations and imperfections we see in our mates are the hardest ones to respond to in grace. Perhaps it's because we think, the smaller a flaw, the more easily it can be changed. Maybe the husband burps loudly when company is present. If his mother didn't teach him good manners, surely he can start learning them now! Maybe the wife has a piercingly shrill voice, and uses it too often to nag her husband. Why can't she be considerate of his overloaded ears, and hold it down a few decibels? The minor flaws most often cause us to whip out our mental performance notebook and record, "You blew it!"

Naturally there are things about Donna that I don't like. And I'm sure, if we each made a list of things we don't like about the other, hers would be the longer! We do not always manage to relate to each other in grace as wonderfully as in the examples I gave. Even so, we love each other dearly, faults and all. If you're thinking that such a love is impossible, in a way you're right. But please stay with me till the end of the chapter. Forgiving love, or grace, does become possible as we let God restructure our attitudes and habits.

Does your wife always burn the toast? Does your husband snore like a chain saw? Did you think you were marrying a Billy Graham or an Elisabeth Elliot, and wake up to find you're stuck with a plain ordinary person like yourself? Is your sincere response, "I love you anyway"?

The Phantom Strikes

If not, perhaps you are not relating to yourself in grace. You may be harping continually at yourself, "I do not measure up to my own standards of what a husband (or wife) should be." Then you have fallen victim to the "phantom syndrome." You have constructed a phantom in your mind—an imaginary perfect person to whom you constantly compare yourself.

For example, I could mentally size myself up against a phantom perfect husband. He's tall, dark and handsome (I'm none of the above). He's a deep student of theology (I'm the gregarious, grab-my-verse-for-the-day-and-run type). He's the perfect father (I think I'm pretty good, but perfect? No way). And so on, until I become paralyzed by an overblown sense of my own inadequacy.

Donna and I watched the phantom syndrome take hold during the early months of our marriage. My previous wife of ten years was taken to be with the Lord through an automobile accident in 1978. So when Donna imagined a phantom perfect wife, she could even give her a name! Gradually Donna realized that my first wife couldn't have been as perfect as she feared. She saw that God had chosen her to be the new wife and mother in our family, and that He wanted to use and work through her. That gave her courage to accept herself in a situation in which she felt very inadequate.

Again, the point is relating in grace — seeing the faults, but loving anyway — even when the person you're relating to is yourself.

Putting others on a performance-standard — "measure up to my expectations if you want me to love you" — often has an even more basic cause. We Christians so easily forget that the Lord deals completely in grace with those who are His. We too often have the attitude my children communicated one morning at breakfast:

Millay (aged 2): "Juice! Want more juice!"

David (aged 3-1/2), quite sternly: "You have to love God first, Millay. If you don't love God, you can't have any juice!"

He Invented "Grace"

In spite of what my children seem to think, the Christian life isn't "Love God, and then you'll get your juice." Rather, out of His heart of forgiving love, God sent Jesus, His dear Son, to be punished cruelly in our place. We should have been put to death for all we've been and done, but Jesus came, stood in front of us and said to God, "I'll take the penalty instead." A Christmas card we received expressed it beautifully: "He came to pay a debt He didn't owe because we owed a debt we couldn't pay."

From the moment we accept that gift of love, we enter into a grace relationship with God the Father. From then on, He says to us, "All your sins have been paid for. I don't want you to sin further, but even when you do, I still love you." When we come to Him, He doesn't merely wipe the slate clean—He throws it away! That's grace.

This should be the foundation of all our other relationships. "We love," the apostle John said, "because He first loved us" (1 John 4:19). A person who never has opened his eyes to see God's love and opened his hands to receive it will scarcely be able to open his arms to receive a marriage partner with full forgiving love.

How do we lay hold of the love we need? Imagine yourself approaching an imposing gilded European palace. In the forecourt stands a large three-tiered marble fountain. Water is bubbling from the top and spilling down into the huge marble bowls beneath. The top bowl represents your inner self. It receives the

28

water first. When it is full, the water splashes over the rim and down to the second level, Which is your spouse. When both upper tiers are full, the water overflows to the third, your children, your closest friends, and so on.

Now, let this image sink into your heart: *The Lord's forgiving love for you is that water, and He is the one pouring it into your life.* Only as you continually open yourself to Him and receive it, will you have real accepting love to spill over to your husband or wife, and on to others around you.

Seeing What's Really There

One of the prettiest pieces of geography on earth, the Black Forest, is quite near our home in West Germany. Donna and I often take our retreats there. We drive higher and higher, past sloping meadows, dense fir forests and green valleys stretching out below.

That scenery in itself is breathtaking. But on a few days a year, on extraordinarily clear days, something magic happens. From the heights, one looks far to the south. There, nearly a hundred miles away, rise those majestic snow-robed kings and queens, the Swiss Alps.

The Alps are always there, soaring silently into the clouds. Yet because of atmospheric haze, they rarely are visible from that distance. It is the same with God's love. He always loves us, with a love so towering that we can never see to the top of it. But the haze of our daily atmosphere often prevents us from catching anything but a faint glimmer of that love in the distance.

"The earth is full of the lovingkindness of the LORD," the psalmist writes (Psalm 33:5, NAS). Yet how seldom we see it! We must ask God to sweep back the clouds and show us His forgiving love which, though often invisible, is always surrounding us. That love is the true basis for all our dealing in grace with other humans.

THE SECOND NUTRIENT: COMMITMENT

A second nutrient basic to the soil of your marriage garden is commitment. Like grace, the meaning of commitment is elusive. For some people, it has become worn and frayed from casual overuse. Others shy away from it altogether; it has a harsh, impenetrable sound.

Again, I find my pocket thesaurus helpful. Looking up *commitment,* I am directed to *promise.* Some of the words listed under promise are: *undertaking, sacred word, pledge, word of honor, vow, profession, guarantee, contract, covenant.*

A Binding Contract

Marriage is an *undertaking* before God. Donna and I have given our *sacred word* that we *pledge* our lives to each other, for as long as we both are on this earth. This is a special *word of honor* which we *vowed* to each other in the public *profession* of our wedding ceremony. We *guaranteed* that we would remain faithful to each other. In our eyes, this ceremony constituted a binding *contract* with each other. We did not mentally cross our fingers behind our backs and think, "This commitment will remain if all goes as I hope it will ... if Donna keeps her youthful figure ... if Roger really gives me the love I need ... if I don't fall for anyone else ... if neither of us becomes handicapped ... if ... if ...." No, We each made a *covenant* and are determined to remain true to it, even if the other partner should disappoint us deeply.

If grace is the proper daily attitude of a marriage relationship, then commitment is like the seal of the will stamped across the whole of it. Commitment is saying, "I *choose* to remain married to you, to devote myself to you. I resolve to meet any hardships head-on, and never to give up. Divorce is not an option. I refuse to admit defeat, to shrug and say, 'It just didn't work out.'"

For the Christian, this should be obvious. When the marriage water gets hot, however, some try to jump out with a spiritual-sounding escape clause: "I guess I married 'out of God's will,' so we'd better get a divorce."

"You Can't Make It Tough Enough"

In 1971, the staff of our organization was getting ready for one of the largest gatherings of Christians, Explo '72. At the Explo office in Dallas, Texas, a team of us worked tirelessly to coordinate the coming together of 80,000 people from all over the United States. Somebody came up with a catchy little saying, which became in effect the motto for the entire congress: "You can't make it tough enough for me to complain."

Even when staff stayed up all night with last-minute preparations? Or when conferees slept on hard floors because the mattresses ran out? Even when they sat through an entire evening's session in the pouring rain? "You can't make it tough enough for me to complain," they said to each other, and they were encouraged to press on.

Does the husband make some foolish investments, ripping away his family's financial security? Is the wife too tired from kids and cleaning to be a livewire in bed? "You can't make it tough enough for me to complain."

That's the mindset of commitment.

45% + 30% = Trouble!

Another category I found under the word *commitment* in my thesaurus was *giving*. In marriage, it's easy to slip into the attitude of "What's in it for me?" That might work if the other partner is an extremely selfless, giving person. What more often happens is that both are determined to put in only their 50 percent, and take out as much as they can. Before long one or the other slips back to 49 percent, then 48. The other retaliates by retreating to 45 percent. The downhill slide has begun.

The only way to have a solid base of commitment is for both partners to want to give 100 percent. I say "want to" because we are weak and fallible. At times one spouse may be going through a crisis and not give much at all. The wife is pregnant, or the husband loses his job. At times we can barely tread water and we need to be given to for a while, in order to regroup. But still the basic attitude of commitment should be there, undergirding the relationship.

Donna and I have talked about what we would do if the other were to become an invalid — or worse, to go into a coma that stretched into years. We haven't come up with any pat answers, but just talking about it has helped us explore the depths of our commitment to each other.

Withstanding the Blows

We saw a television sports clip from a basketball game the other day that had us laughing out loud. Team A had the ball and dribbled down the court through the defenses of Team B. A space opened, and the forward with the ball ran up to dunk it. When the ball slammed into the metal rim, the unbelievable happened. At the impact of the ball, the entire backboard exploded and disintegrated into a zillion pieces of plastic dust.

Commitment in marriage is like a backboard. It must be strong, solid, able to withstand the blows that will come. When a couple says, "We'll give marriage a try and see what happens," disintegration is only a matter of time. It was hilarious to see the powdered plastic sifting all over the players' heads and onto the glossy hardwood floor. It's not so amusing, however, to watch a marriage shatter into a useless heap of dust.

Like grace, commitment can grow and deepen as a couple allows God's forgiving love to pour into their lives.

THE THIRD NUTRIENT: THE HOLY SPIRIT

By this time you may be thinking, *Relating in grace and total commitment are wonderful ideas, but just how will we manage all that?* The key is found in the third basic ingredient—the work of the Holy Spirit in your marriage.

Without the energizing power of the Holy Spirit, a marriage will be as lifeless as a garden of plastic flowers. With His presence, it can be growing and vital, bringing much praise to God. It is He who helps us experience God's love as a daily reality. But who is the Holy Spirit? How do we know if He is present? And how can we see Him work in the humdrum of our everyday lives?

He's Not "The Force"

First of all, the Holy Spirit is not an "it." He is neither a wraith-like creature nor an impersonal power like "The Force" in *Star Wars*. Rather, He is a person, the third person of the Trinity: Father, Son and Holy Spirit. The qualities possessed by God the Father and Jesus Christ the Son are His also.

In John 14, when Jesus told His disciples that He would be leaving them, He explained that someone else would come to them, to help and encourage them. He was referring to the Holy Spirit. In a sense then, the Holy Spirit is Jesus' representative here on earth at the present time. His task is to testify about Jesus (John 15:26), to bring glory to the Son (John 16:14) and to help us understand God's Word (John 14:26). The Holy Spirit gives Christians the power to live in obedience to Christ. Without His active working in our hearts, our attempts at living Christian lives would result in hopeless failure.

But Is He There?

How can you know if the Holy Spirit is present in your marriage? The Bible teaches that God's Spirit is present in a person's heart from the moment he trusts in Christ (1 Corinthians 6:19). At that instant, the individual is sealed in Christ by the Holy Spirit for all eternity (Ephesians 1:13-14). If you are not certain whether you've ever really placed your faith in Christ, this is a good time to make sure. You can tell Him you want to do so with a simple prayer, such as the following:

Lord Jesus, I need You. Thank You for dying on the cross for my sins. I open the door of my life and receive You as my Savior and Lord. Thank You for forgiving my sins and giving me eternal life. Take control of my life. Make me the kind of person You want me to be.

Some Christians are convinced that the Holy Spirit is not present anywhere in their lives. If He were, how could they be living as they are?

They need to understand that there may be a great difference between the *fact* of the Spirit's presence within them and the *experience* of His influence over them. The presence of a skilled teacher in a classroom doesn't guarantee that thirty unruly students will be under his control. In the same way, the presence of the Holy Spirit in one's heart doesn't guarantee that all the unruly elements of the life are under His dominion.

In a recent article in *Worldwide Challenge* magazine, Dr. Bill Bright, founder of Campus Crusade for Christ International, compared the average Christian to a man struggling to swim upstream against a strong current. The Christian who tries to live life in the power of his own resources surely feels exactly like that. He swims as hard as he can just to stay in one place! On the other hand, the Christian who connects to the Holy Spirit's unlimited power supply is like a person riding up that same raging stream in a motor boat.

Completing the Connection

How do we make contact with the power supply that is available to us? I travel a lot and spend many nights each year in European hotels that vary from semi-seedy to quite respectable. Whatever their quality, I always find an outlet for my electric shaver in the bathroom near the mirror.

How am I able to shave each morning? First of all, I have the right kind of electric shaver, one which works on European current. If I plug it in, there will not likely be an explosion. You might say that, having ordered the room and possessing the proper shaver, I have the *right* at any time to plug it in and use it. The hotel management expects me to use it.

As Christians, we belong to Christ and have the Holy Spirit living within us. Therefore, we don't need to beg God to give us His Spirit. We have Him already. God the Father has set up everything for us, expecting that we will make use of His power.

Second, I have implicit trust (however poorly based) in the hotel management and electrical supply system of the city. I never have wondered if the current will be there. I merely plug it in and shave. In other words, I have *faith*.

The Christian who has faith is aware of God's overwhelming love, as explained earlier in this chapter. He knows that God wants to give us power and joy through His Spirit, instead of leaving us wallowing in our frustrations. The person who is sure of these facts can trust that the supply of current, the Spirit's power, will be available to him.

What is Filling Us?

Ephesians 5:18 gives us a graphic image of what it means to let God's Spirit supply the power for our lives. In this verse Paul writes, "And do not get drunk with wine ... but be filled with the Spirit" (NAS). Picture it: An inebriated man, his eyes staring blankly into space and his body movements no longer under his own control, rolls out of his chair onto the floor. What is "filling" or controlling him? Alcohol.

We see the contrast in Ephesians 5:19: "singing and making melody with your heart to the Lord" (NAS). Who is filling this person, determining the direction of his life, giving him the desire and power to live? The Holy Spirit. The meaning of the Greek in verse 18 is "keep on being filled" with the Spirit. It is something I need to ask God for repeatedly, as I sense something else has begun to fill me and crowd Him out. In *The Simplicity of the Spirit-Filled Life,* L.L. Legters writes:

> Why should God link being drunken with wine with being filled with the Spirit? I think it must have been in order that the most unlearned would know how to be filled. Every child in Paul's day knew that a person was filled with wine by drinking wine, and that to remain filled he kept on drinking. Even so the only way by which one can be filled with the Spirit is by drinking, and to remain filled one continues drinking.[1]

(For further treatment of this topic, refer to the reprint of Dr. Bright's booklet on the Spirit-filled life in appendix C at the end of this book.)

If I ask God to fill me with His Spirit, will my life undergo a sudden, dramatic change? Perhaps not. A classroom full of disobedient students hardly will be subdued in just one class period. It takes time for a teacher to win respect and to bring all the disruptive class members under the rule of his authority. Likewise, I should not expect an instant and total change of character when I ask God to fill me with His Spirit. As much as I might wish it, it rarely happens! But over the years, as I consistently confess my failures to God and ask Him to fill me again, I do see new life patterns gradually replacing the old.

Not A Do-It-Yourself Project

It is a natural human tendency to want to do everything ourselves and to give up control only when we have no other choice. I expect that God is delighted, though, when we turn to Him long before we're at wit's end. Surely He who designed our intricate lives is more than ready to give us his plans for them. "I know the plans that I have for you, declares the LORD, plans for welfare and not for calamity, to give you a future and a hope," (Jeremiah 29:11,NAS). Only as we rely on His Spirit living within us will these plans be carried out. That includes the wonderful plans He has for our walk with our earthly mate.

Bringing It All Together

Grace, commitment, the Holy Spirit — the soil of a healthy marriage garden will be suffused with these elements. An illustration from my first marriage shows how the three elements can intertwine to form a foundation for growth.

When my first wife, Lynn, was killed, it seemed as if half of my own person had been ripped from me. During our ten years of marriage, she had become to me the dearest person in all the world.

Yet it wasn't always that way. We married just out of college, full of hopes and also full of unrealistic expectations. Not many months passed before the honeymoon glow faded, and we both realized that our expectations of the other person were not being fulfilled. We each had in mind certain minimum standards for the other. To our dismay, not even those were being met!

In spite of the fact that we were in "the Lord's work," we were immature. We each secretly depended on marriage to meet our own needs, rather than seeing it as a chance to meet the needs of the other.

When I saw that Lynn was giving only 45 percent to our marriage, instead of the necessary 50, I retaliated by pulling back to 40 percent. That hurt her, and she pulled back to 35. And so it went. It was anything *but* a grace relationship!

About two years into our marriage, Lynn no longer could cope emotionally with my aloofness. "Divorce" began to come up in our hurtful conversations. It became a familiar word, which each week came closer to becoming reality. "If this is all there is," she finally announced one day, "then I want out." It was no hasty statement; she meant it. She left and moved into a motel for a few days to get some distance between us. Sad to say, if I hadn't been a full-time Christian worker, I gladly would have given her what she asked for.

During this crisis, I at last was willing to humble myself enough to read a book on Christian marriage and to get some counsel from a friend. I came to the conviction that for us, divorce was absolutely no option. When Lynn returned, I expressed to her my commitment to our marriage in the strongest terms. Something in my new attitude encouraged her that there was hope for us, and we turned the corner. If divorce wasn't an option, the only other choice was to take what little we had and trust God to show us how to make it better.

Back to the Basics

Together, we turned back to the basics of what we had been taught (and ironically, were teaching others!) — the Spirit-led life. We subtly had drifted away from soaking ourselves in God's Word, so that He could refresh our attitudes. Once we returned to that, we discovered that our prayers no longer were like stale leftovers. They were fresh and new. We were learning all over again what it means to "abide in Christ" (John 15) and to "live by the Spirit" (Galatians 5).

Essentials

We also had to turn to the Holy Spirit for the ability to start loving each other again. Our feelings had been deeply wounded, and they didn't change overnight. But we knew that the fruit of the Spirit is love (Galatians 5:22). We needed love, so we claimed it as something we knew God wanted us to have. Slowly and gradually, it became real in our lives. We began to relate to one another in grace.

It took several years before we could honestly say, "We have a good, strong marriage now." But we were moving forward all the time.

Lynn and I had put each other under a performance standard. Because we had not responded to each other in grace, we had drifted further and further apart. It took a renewal of our marriage commitment to bring us together again. We also needed the Holy Spirit's power to live with each other in forgiving love.

A flourishing, healthy marriage is just not possible without *grace* (forgiving love) and unshakable *commitment*. And these are hardly achievable, except in a superficial way, without the undergirding power from God's energy source, the *Holy Spirit*.

These are deep topics, which I've only touched upon lightly. I hope I've whetted your appetite to dig further into some of the books suggested in the bibliography. We'll return to the concepts presented in this chapter again and again.

Getting Ready To Go

With these nutrients nourishing the soil of your relationship, you are ready for a productive getaway. But maybe you've also noticed some rocks in the garden, some obstacles which first need to be removed.

You may have some well-founded fears: "Will my spouse agree to this crazy dream of a weekend away? If so, will we be able to open up? What if we open up too much and are misunderstood and hurt? Whatever will we do and say, with hours stretching out endlessly before us?"

Perhaps, on the other hand, your objections are purely practical. "Who on earth would want our kids for a whole weekend? Where could we go that wouldn't break our already strained budget?"

I'll address these kinds of questions in chapter 4. I hope that by the end of that chapter, you'll be saying, "I think this getaway is something we can manage." I encourage you to go for it!

Chapter 4
Chuck Those Rocks Over the Fence

In back of our house, we have a small vegetable garden. This is completely Donna's responsibility. She's the one who likes to kneel in the soil with the sun on her back and get her fingernails dirty.

Once a year, however, she persuades me to help her turn over all the earth in our little patch. Each time an amazing number of rocks surfaces. As these stones emerge, we simply toss them over the fence into the field behind our house. But we never are rid of them completely. (I'm convinced that they mulitiply when we're not looking!)

Likewise, when you begin to consider a marriage retreat, you may have to remove some obstacles. The first part of this chapter deals with two main "boulders" that can hinder you from ever taking a marriage retreat. Next are the "pebbles"— the practical questions of how and where to get away. Then, in the final section, you'll have a chance to sit down together to map out the specifics of your retreat. You'll decide how, where and when, and even more important, *what* topics you will choose to cover.

DIGGING OUT BOULDERS

Taking The Plunge

It's quite likely that one of you is enthusiastic over the idea of a marriage getaway, while the other is lukewarm or negative. The objection may be much more fundamental than merely doubting that you can afford it and fit it into your schedule. One or both of you may be uneasy about facing the negatives that a few hours of in-depth interaction could unearth. This apprehension might be the first boulder you encounter.

I can't deny it: Coming to grips with truth can be painful. Closets may be wrenched open, revealing grisly skeletons. But do not allow the fear of these unpleasant disclosures to stifle your weekend before it even has a chance to get started.

Preparation As newlyweds, Donna and I enjoyed our first few retreats, but we never talked about any serious matters. Why? Because I was just flat scared, too scared to be vulnerable. I figured that opening up and admitting to Donna that I wasn't the spiritual leader I wanted to be, or that I was struggling in the area of self-discipline, would be like a duck telling a hunter it was open season. I was sure she'd gun me down, leaving my self-esteem a bullet-riddled carcass.

On about the third weekend away, my (by then somewhat frustrated) wife delicately insisted that we do something besides eat out and sleep. With deep misgivings (which I was too proud to acknowledge), I agreed to discuss some in-depth questions that we'd brought along. I was amazed to discover that Donna didn't try to impale me on the thorns of my own deficiencies. Instead, we had a candid and encouraging time of brainstorming about how we could assist each other in areas of weakness.

We realized that communication is the essence of a marriage retreat. As our convictions about communication grew stronger, Donna and I determined to write this handbook to help other couples. Our efforts are in vain, however, if, for fear of opening up to each other, you never take the first step of getting away.

Basis for Being Vulnerable

Before we can improve our practical skills of communication, we must lay the foundation. What is this foundation? *It is the assurance that the other person won't reject me if I share my very soul. It's knowing that, even if what I reveal of myself is negative, the other person can handle it.*

Why is this so hard? In his book, *The Trauma of Transparency*, J. Grant Howard points to the natural human desire to be perfect as a major hindrance to communication. Of course, we are not perfect, but our pride would have us conceal that fact. If we don't open up, we won't lose face with our spouses! Maybe we can pull the wool over our own eyes, too. If we don't share our real (imperfect) selves, we may forget that those imperfections even exist.

All of this is very safe, in the same way that a body in a coffin is safe from any of the risks of pain, fear or discomfort that living beings can experience. It's also very dead!

Opening up with one's spouse can be scary, but the rewards are many. And honest communication can begin when both are convinced that, even if their mates feel hurt or upset over an unpleasant revelation, they will not start packing their bags.

Because Donna and I have this confidence, we can communicate honestly. I don't mean that we feel compelled to reveal every negative thought that crosses our minds. But when we need to talk about our below-the-surface selves, we can do so without fear of losing the other's love and commitment.

How is this possible? We dare to expose our true selves to each other, because we know that our marriage belongs to the Lord Jesus Christ. He is the author of both of us and of our marriage. He ultimately is responsible for how we turn out as individuals and as a unit. Knowing that puts our whole relationship into the realm of faith. It becomes what is sometimes termed a "faith marriage."

The Third Strand

"A cord of three strands is not easily broken," Solomon wrote (Ecclesiastes 4:12, NAS). Before our wedding, Donna and I saw many marriages breaking apart because of a lack of that third strand.

So we began searching for wedding bands which would be daily reminders, especially when times got tough, that the Lord Himself was the third party in our union. After weeks of looking and then committing the matter to God in prayer, we finally found rings made of three intertwining strands, illustrating that the Lord binds us together in His love.

If you are believers in Jesus Christ, He *is* the third strand in your marriage. He binds you together. No matter what your backgrounds, if you are married now, you can trust that Jesus Christ is for your marriage. He's on your side. He wants you to accept your mate as from His hand. He wants your relationship to succeed, and He can make it succeed, if you both let Him.

But how does this relate to communication? We must understand God's active part in our marriages if we are to begin to talk freely with our mates. As we become convinced that the Lord is the central, binding strand in our relationships, only then can we relax, drop our defenses and let our partner get a glimpse into our heart. As we understand that we have a faith marriage, *resting not on our own adequacy, but on the faithfulness of God,* we can heave over the fence boulder number one: the fear of being open and vulnerable in communicating with each other.

Preparation

A Faith Step

Now for boulder number two. Another possible hindrance to getting away together is that one spouse simply doesn't feel the need for it. One partner is chomping at the bit, while the other is asking, "What's the big deal?"

To the mate in the first category, I'd advise the soft sell. Express your desire to get away and the benefits that you visualize. Have some ideas in mind for financing and babysitting (see the last part of this chapter.) Check chapter 6 for some ideas on communicating your needs openly, yet lovingly.

To the reluctant partner, I'd encourage you to see the getaway as a step of faith. If it will meet some emotional needs for your mate, it's a small price to pay. I have learned that I am happiest when my wife is happy. When I choose to do something that encourages her, the benefits invariably return to me. In 1 Corinthians 7, wives and husbands are exhorted to meet each other's sexual needs, even if they don't feel like it at the time. I believe that we should not deprive each other emotionally, either, when we have the ability to give.

A marriage retreat might need to be such a "gift" to your spouse. You might say, "Honey, I don't feel the need for this right now, but if it's that important to you, I'm willing to step out and go. I trust that the Lord will take this weekend and use it to our benefit." That puts your getaway into the realm of faith. And every retreat truly must be a faith weekend, a weekend in which the Lord must be active for anything significant to occur.

SOME PRACTICAL PEBBLES

Coming Up With the Cash

Now let's turn our attention to some practical considerations: finances, location and babysitting.

The first question is: *How can we finance our getaway?* If one mate sees this problem more clearly than the other, things could get a bit tense, as in the following:

SHE: "We never get enough time alone. Why don't we get away for a weekend?"

HE: (Sees $$) "We just can't afford that right now."

SHE: (Hears REJECTION) "Why do you always avoid being alone with me?"

HE: (Feeling trapped) "Why does whatever you want to do always cost money?"

SHE: (Feeling totally rejected) "Money, money, money! You just don't even care about our marriage, do you!"

HE: (Visualizes $$ thrown in the trash) "O.K., O.K., we'll go. I suppose you wanna go to the Hilton, right?"

In this illustration, the wife "won" . . . sort of. But I'm afraid that even if this couple does get away, unless they first work through this issue, their time together won't be very fruitful.

The husband in the above dialogue had a legitimate concern: A weekend away might be expensive. The wife could have helped alleviate that concern with some creative ideas on how to come up with the money. The following are a few suggestions:

1. Ask for the weekend as a Christmas or birthday gift from your spouse or parents. Or decide to make it your joint anniversary gift this year.
2. Use your income tax refund. (If you had to pay extra taxes this year, forget I mentioned it!)
3. Have a garage sale or yard sale and earmark the proceeds for your getaway.
4. Decide not to eat out for several months, and deliberately set aside the money you would have spent. Or purposely put off buying some extras you've been wanting.
5. Dip into your savings account. You'll reap dividends from this weekend for the rest of your lives.

Preparation

I am confident that after your first marriage retreat, you'll be so delighted with the benefits to your relationship that you'll work it into your yearly budget as a matter of course.

A Tent or the Hilton?

Preparation

The above ideas are based on the assumption that a certain amount of cash is available to you. For the couple who really is pinching pennies, though, a getaway is still possible. Let's look at our second question: *Where could we go?* Some of the suggestions here are as cheap as staying at home:

1. Arrange with another couple to trade homes for a weekend (with your children farmed out elsewhere, of course!). It may not be the Hilton, but it gets you out of your own cage. Be sure to unplug the phones. Give the phone number of the other couple's next-door neighbor to your babysitter, in case of emergency.

2. You may know somebody with a cabin in the mountains or at the beach. Ask if you could borrow it for a few days during the off-season. Offer to pay the utilities, and of course, leave the place spotless. Don't feel that you can't "beg"—that's false pride. Most Christians with such possessions are delighted to serve the Lord through them. They especially are apt to be willing if you explain the purpose of your weekend. They may want to take a marriage retreat themselves!

3. Borrow camping equipment, if you don't have your own, and head for the hills. Or rent a cabin at a nearby state or national park. (Off-season is preferable.) Don't plan to drive too far, though, because it cuts into your communication time. Of course, if you camp out, you are at the mercy of the weather, but even that is not a problem. If you're trapped in your tent in the rain, just think how much you can talk!

4. Check with the Chamber of Commerce or local tourist information to see if country inns are in your area. These probably would provide a more scenic, restful setting, and perhaps cost less.

5. If you really don't feel you've gotten "away" unless you go to a nice hotel, start checking your newspaper. Many first-class city hotels offer very inexpensive weekend specials.

Ideas one through three have a possible disadvantage of tying the wife down to the stove, just as she is at home. If you choose such an option, try to eat at least one meal a day out, and bring sandwiches for the others.

Personally, I prefer to borrow a cabin in the mountains or stay at a country inn. City hotels can be noisy and confining. Since moving to Europe, Donna and I have learned the art of communicating on foot. We usually take our retreats at a small country hotel with plenty of scenic footpaths nearby. As our blood circulation gets stimulated, so does our conversation! We take along a pocket-sized notebook and pen to jot down ideas that come to us on our strolls.

Who'll Keep the Kids?

A third possible pebble in planning a retreat is the *need for a qualified babysitter*. It is very important, especially for the wife's sake (not to mention for the kids' sake!) to have a babysitting arrangement with which you are comfortable. If you're not in the habit of leaving your kids, this will be another step of faith—maybe a giant one. When times are hectic, we sometimes hesitate to take a retreat, feeling that our children need our presence. Actually, what they need even more is for us to invest a couple of days in clearly thinking through our relationships with each other and with them, so that the family "ship" can sail more smoothly. The Lord, who wants you to have the blessing of this time away together, certainly can make sure your children won't suffer as a result. Here are some possibilities:

1. Find one or two singles, or a married couple without children, who'd be willing to stay in your home while you're gone. Offer to pay them a reasonable amount, but they probably will see it more as a ministry to you than as a way to make money.
2. Encourage another couple with children to take a marriage retreat, and offer to trade off keeping each others' kids. (Pick somebody with well-behaved children!)
3. Send your children to visit their grandparents.
4. Have the grandparents keep the children at your home. When we've done this, we have had our regular teenage babysitter on tap to ease the load, or had a single girl stay at the house, also.

5. Send each child to a friend's home, with an offer to each mother to reciprocate.
6. Take a nursing baby with you. This is not ideal, but it's definitely better than not getting away at all. (If the baby is colicky, forget it!)

These are our best ideas for finances, location and babysitters. You probably will think of others, as you consider your particular situation.

Preparation

TALK-TIME

The next step is a pre-retreat "talk time." This will provide an opportunity to air any lingering hesitations about taking a marriage retreat, and to plan the details.

Set aside one evening to be alone together. Put the kids to bed early, unplug the phones, turn off the television, and talk through the questions on the next few pages. If you prefer to go out, look for a quiet place where you can spend a couple of hours without being shooed off to make room for more customers. This talk time will be a vital key to the success of your marriage retreat. Read the following questions aloud and discuss them. Make notes as necessary to plan for your retreat. Try not to get embroiled in deep discussions; save those for your getaway!

Your First Retreat

If you have not previously taken a marriage retreat, each take a sheet of paper and briefly answer the following questions. Write your feelings first; then discuss what you have written.

1. *When I think about taking a marriage retreat, I feel . . .*

   because . . .

2. *I would prefer to go for*
   an entire weekend
   one overnight
   one day, without overnight.
   My reasons:

When, Who, How and Where

1. *When would be the best weekend* (or overnight, or day)? (List three choices, to be decided based on availability of baby sitters.)
2. *Who will keep the children?* (List several options.)
3. *How will we get the money?* (List three possibilities.)
4. *Where will we go?* (List several options, and decide who will make the necessary phone calls.)

Now for the "What"

It's time to think about what you and your spouse will cover on your upcoming retreat. You probably will want to take future getaways, so don't feel pressured to deal with all of the topics in chapters 6 to 12 in one gulp. We'll discuss a little later how to break them into bite-sized pieces.

Pick Your Topics

First, take this survey to help you pinpoint areas of need. If the statement in quotations has a familiar ring, check the box beside it.

☐ 1. *"When it comes to communicating, one of us is a Niagara Falls and the other is a silent Sphinx. I wish we could learn to talk openly."*

☐ 2. *"Surely a Christian marriage is more than two believers being wed. We need more spiritual interaction."*

☐ 3. *"They say opposites attract, but with all our differences, I don't know how we keep from flying apart. The only thing we have in common is that we both hate mayonnaise!"*

☐ 4. *"My wife used to be a livewire in bed, but lately I think she's blown a fuse. We sure can't talk about it, either!"*

☐ 5. *"Every day is like fruit-basket turnover around our house. We started our married life with some great dreams, but none of them have ever come true."*

☐ 6. *"My husband saves used toothpicks. He almost had to be hospitalized after I bought the fur coat. If he'd show me more love through gifts, I wouldn't have to buy them myself!"*

☐ 7. *"Our kids are little monkeys, and our home is becoming a zoo!"*

☐ 8. *"It's nice to belong to a church that teaches God's Word, but I seem to just sit, soak and sour. Surely the Lord didn't leave us on earth to be Christian spectators."*

☐ 9. *"We've been on some great marriage retreats in the past, but everything evaporates once we hit the front door at home. We need to know how we can make it last."*

Preparation   Each of the problems above corresponds to a chapter that follows. For example, if you checked statement number one, then you might want to begin your retreat by interacting on chapter 6, which addresses no-barriers communication. Correlate your survey responses with the following explanation of the chapters. Then decide together which topics you want to discuss on your proposed retreat. This advanced planning is essential, as questions will be provided, but not many answers! Therefore, you will find it helpful to take along extra resource material.

The following are some suggested chapters to interact on, and some additional questions to discuss, according to the question numbers you checked above:

Question

1...Chapter 6, "Open Your Cans of Worms"
   Why is no-barriers communication so important in marriage? What are some techniques that can help us achieve it?

2...Chapter 7, "Mortar in Your Garden Wall"
   What is "spiritual oneness," and why is it important? How can we become closer spiritually?

3...Chapter 8, "You Get the Shovel; I'll Take the Rake"
   What am I like? And my mate? How do we interrelate in various areas? How can we live with our differences? How can we build up each other?

4...Chapter 9, "Your Vines Intertwining"
   How can we achieve greater intimacy? How can we help our lovemaking become more fulfilling for both of us?

5...Chapter 10, "Green Thumbs Make Blueprints"
   How can we live according to our priorities, so that our dreams become realities? Or, if we've never had any dreams, how can we develop some?

6...Chapter 11, Finances:
What are our material values? How can we keep our financial ship afloat?

7...Chapter 12, "Nurturing Your Young Olive Plants"
What qualities should characterize our particular family? How can we help our children and teenagers grow into maturity? How can we have special family times?

8...Chapter 13, "The Fruit That Won't Rot"
How can we, as a couple, minister to others? What if we don't feel capable or qualified?

9...Chapter 14, "Subdue Those Weekly Weeds"
How can we work all the wonderful ideas from our marriage retreat into our hectic daily lives?

If you're planning a weekend away, that is, about two days (Friday night through Sunday night), then choose not more than three areas to cover. If you're taking only one day, pick not more than two. You may find that you have time for only one. Save the rest for your next escape!

Consider spending your first retreat working through chapters 6, 7, and 8, in that order. Good communication, spiritual unity and mutual understanding are foundational. You might be surprised at how much you can resolve in another area (sexual intimacy, for example) by studying those basic topics.

After you've made your choices, note the chapter numbers of the topics you've decided to cover on your weekend. Then check the bibliography. Pick a couple of books or cassettes on each subject you have chosen and skim through them before you go. Mark sections of the books to be read aloud with your partner on the retreat.

I'd like to stress the importance of taking along a few resources that can help you focus on God's perspective. Going on a faith retreat means you are counting on God to meet with you and reveal how your marriage can better glorify Him. Therefore, taking along some proven spiritual guidance is vital.

The whole retreat concept is very flexible and should be adapted to meet your particular needs. Some couples who field-tested this book were not able to get away overnight during a three-month period. Instead, they set aside time in the evenings after the children were in bed. One couple even made use of a long car trip together to discuss their topics! Here are examples of how three different couples might use the material in this workbook.

Couple A

 Mark and Jenny never had taken a retreat before and they had checked several boxes on the survey. First, they sensed that their relationship with each other was not very smooth. Jenny got easily irritated at Mark, to which he responded by withdrawing. They also admitted that their sex life hadn't been very good since the baby was born. And they continually fight over where their money goes.

 After talking it over, Mark and Jenny (very wisely, I think!) decided to cover Chapters 6 through 8, in that order, even though they *felt* they had more needs in the area of intimacy and finances. They realized that there wasn't much point in skipping over the basics. They marked several books from the bibliography that could give them good background information on the topics they chose. Jenny borrowed the books from the church library and skimmed them before they left on their retreat.

Couple B

 Dave and Michelle have been on productive marriage retreats in the past. This time they can get away only for one day. They want to use the time to discuss needs and plans for each of their three children, so they'll work through chapter 11. Sarah, the middle child, has been showing many signs of anxiety and insecurity lately. They've just bought a copy of Dr. James Dobson's *Hide or Seek* and plan to read it before they go. They also want to review chapter 14, so that they can get back to having their weekly talk times.

Couple C

 Bob and Sandy can't manage a retreat until six months from now, but they have a hot topic: Should they ask Bob's ailing mother to move in with them? They will take an evening out next week to discuss this. They'll look in chapter 14 under the heading, "How to Handle a Hot Topic." In the same chapter they'll also find some ideas for developing weekly talk times, to tide them over until the longer getaway.

 Do you see how adaptable this is? You take what you need

Preparation

and cover what you have time for. You use the marriage retreat as part of an ongoing process of coming together in thorough, creative discussion of the facets of your marriage and family life.

So...get going! And don't forget to take along:

— your retreat "Talkbook" (A medium-sized looseleaf ring binder, with notebook dividers and plenty of blank paper.) This should be a nice binder, of good quality, as it will become your permanent chronological retreat record book. Add more dividers as you work through new areas.

— your Bibles (two or three different versions)

— reference books

— possibly a cassette player, with praise music tapes and message cassettes related to your topics

— your Whoopee Kit, if you're staying overnight (i.e., candles, bubblebath, a lacy nighty, etc.)

— this handbook (see chapter 5 as soon as you arrive at your retreat)

— your calendars, to help put ideas into action

Preparation

Donna and I are praying that couples who take these retreats will have life-changing experiences, which will bring much honor to God. May your getaway do just that!

On Location

Chapter 5

Stake Out Your Boundaries

At last! The kids are taken care of, you've driven to your escape spot and you're finally alone.

Unpack your bags, then sit down to think about what you want to see happen over the next few hours or days. You've gone to a lot of trouble and probably some expense to get this far. So make your time count!

First, put your retreat firmly into the hands of the Master Designer of your marriage. He is delighted that you've taken this step of faith. Now He wants you to see your weekend (or day or date) in the light of faith. You have certain ideas about what should happen during this time. Maybe some of these expectations will be fulfilled—maybe none of them will be! Your job right now is to relax, to trust that God knows what kind of retreat you need, and to leave the results to Him.

I recommend that before you begin your intense time of communication, you each take a "throne-check." Simply ask yourself, who is on the "throne" of my life right now, self or the Holy Spirit? This would be a good time to review Bill Bright's booklet on the Spirit-filled life, reprinted in appendix C.

If you sense that self has taken over, especially if you're "on the outs" with your mate, then "breathe spiritually":

Exhale: First confess to God and then, if necessary, to your mate.

Inhale: Again surrender your throne to the Holy Spirit. Thank God that He will direct and empower you, as He has promised.

You might want to stop here and pray together along the following lines:

Lord, we want to come to You with our hearts open. You are free to make of this time what You want. We need to see Your hand at work in several areas of our lives. Guide our time; help us to use it wisely.

Boundaries

Remind yourselves that this is only the first of many getaways together. When Donna and I were newly married, we were in a state of near exhaustion because so many things were demanded of us. On our first two marriage retreats, all we did was eat and sleep. As I mentioned earlier, this was partly due to my fear of being vulnerable. In retrospect, however, I see that we desperately needed that rest. Because we've had such fruitful times since then, I'm not bothered that we "didn't accomplish a thing" on the earlier ones. Yet, I trust that you will accomplish a thing or two and also relax and have fun. Now get out your loose-leaf notebook and title the first page, "Marriage Retreat, (date)." (If you did not bring a notebook with you, you can purchase one now.) Then make a tentative retreat schedule, leaving a blank beside the times you'll have for intensive talking. Some people cannot converse while eating. If you can, you may also block some of your mealtimes for discussion.

Here's how your schedule might look:

SAMPLE SCHEDULE

Friday   - 7 p.m. - Out to dinner
             8 p.m. - Planning our weekend (this chapter is a guideline)
             9 p.m. - Whoopee night!

Saturday - Sleep in! Remember, this is supposed to be fun!
             9 a.m. - Breakfast (in your room, if possible)
             9:30 - 10 a.m. - Praise and prayer time (this chapter has some ideas)
             10 a.m. - noon - _____
             12 noon - Lunch
             1:30 p.m. - Nap, if needed
             2:30 - 6:30 p.m. - _____
             (Break up this with a walk in a park or by going out for coffee, etc.)

```
            7 p.m. - Out to dinner
            8:30 - 10 p.m. - _____
Sunday   - 9 a.m. - Breakfast
            9:30 a.m. - Praise and prayer time
            10 a.m. - 1 p.m. -_____
            1 p.m. - Lunch
            2 p.m. - Nap, if needed
            3 - 5 p.m. - RETREAT WRAP-UP (see chapter 13)
            Head for home!
```

How does all this work? Wherever you have drawn a line, now write in pencil the name of the topic you plan to discuss during that time slot and the page number of its corresponding chapter in this book. For starters, write in one topic per blank, and re-adjust as you go. (Couples who field-tested this material spent anywhere from one and a half to five hours on each topic!) Be prepared to flex. The purpose of the schedule is not to restrict, but to help you use your time wisely.

Chapters 6 through 13 each begin with straight content, followed by the workbook section. Begin your discussions by reading aloud the chapter's introduction. Continue reading aloud, stopping for interaction, Bible study, affirmation or prayer, when guided by the appropriate symbols. Change readers every so often for variety. Any initial awkwardness you feel in reading to one another probably will diminish as you move further into the book. (Reading aloud is nearly a lost art, but it is coming back in vogue as a way to foster family togetherness.)

In the workbook section, you will find the following symbols:

 Interaction

Read aloud the questions and discuss (or write, as indicated) your answers. If you are communicating openly, you can expect some surprises and maybe some hurt feelings. That's normal! (Chapter 6 offers ideas on communicating in love and on handling anger.)

 Bible Study

Open your Bibles to the passage listed. Read the verses aloud, discuss the questions given, and make notes of your insights. Please don't skip this step! God's Word can hew out new channels of thought and action.

Affirmation

This is a chance for you to affirm each other, to pause in what may be a heavy discussion and say, "You mean a lot to me." While you may want to use your own words, don't omit this opportunity to build up your mate and keep your discussion moving in a positive direction.

 Prayer

Boundaries

Two or three times in each chapter you'll find an opportunity to commit your dialogue to your Heavenly Father in prayer. Naturally your own words are the best, but whatever words you use, do pray! Make a habit of closing any intense discussion, on a retreat or anywhere, by placing it in His hands. The suggested prayers are left open-ended, so that you can close by making them unique to yourselves.

 Action Point

At the end of the chapter, look back over the questions you've discussed and the notes in your Talkbook. You may have generated many ideas; now, try to pick the most important one and decide how to put it into action.

As you interact, keep your loose-leaf Talkbook handy to record ideas, questions and plans. Move at your own pace, even if it's much slower than you had hoped.

If you go away for a weekend and find yourself talking about only one thing, DON'T SWEAT IT! That's probably exactly what you needed to do.

Let's see how "Couple A," Mark and Jenny, used the above proposed schedule.

When they saw that Friday night was set aside for "whoopee," they just shrugged. They knew they had some tensions to resolve first. So they started their Topic #1 (no-barriers communication) on Friday night and continued it on Saturday morning. After their nap on Saturday, they got into Topic #2 (spiritual oneness). They were amazed to discover how many of their irritations seemed to be dissolving already. They sensed that they were learning a lot about what had been causing their marital stress. They began to look forward to their whoopee time that evening!

By 5 p.m., Mark and Jenny were mentally and emotionally exhausted. They had talked more intensely in one twenty-four-hour period than they had done in the past several months. So they decided to a take a break and go window-shopping until time for dinner.

On Sunday morning, they began to deal with Topic #3 (understanding each other). It soon became clear that they weren't going to take care of that in one morning, especially when they hit the heading "Who's in Charge Here?" Emotionally they weren't ready to uncap any volcanoes. So during their Retreat Wrap-up Sunday afternoon, they planned an extended talk time on the following Sunday, to continue working through Topic #3.

Boundaries

What did Mark and Jenny do during the Praise and Prayer Time each morning? First they listened to some songs on the Christian music cassettes they had brought along. They selected those that set an atmosphere of worship. Next they took turns reading aloud a psalm, that helped them praise God.

Then they talked to Him. Neither of them felt very comfortable about praying out loud, but they knew they were God's children. So they spoke to Him as sincerely as they knew how, thanking Him and telling Him of their needs. They had made good progress.

So much for Mark and Jenny. Now how about you? You've staked out some boundaries for your own discussion and put them into a tentative schedule. Remember to keep it flexible, making sure it's meeting your needs. Also, don't forget to wrap up your time with chapter 14.

I'm convinced that God has great things in store for you!

Chapter 6

Open Your Cans of Worms

Communication

When Donna and the children first began to dig in our little garden, I heard frequent cries of "Eek! Look! A yucky worm—get him out of here!" City slickers that we are, we didn't realize until some time later that earthworms are good news in a garden. They loosen the soil so that the roots of the growing plants can spread more freely.

The same is true in marriage. When a husband and wife try to communicate heart-to-heart, suddenly they find they've opened a few cans of worms. The little squiggly creatures start crawling out into the light, and the immediate natural reaction is a loud shriek of disgust.

"Yuck!" both partners exclaim. "Maybe we don't want to be so vulnerable with each other after all." At that point they often quickly shove the worms back into the cans, reseal them and vow to spend the rest of their married lives on guard. They'd rather have a comfortable, non-threatening relationship that doesn't go very deep, than to risk what might crawl out if they open up with each other.

Such couples have a "safe relationship." The partners have learned to suppress their true feelings. Instead of confronting their mates and dealing with a negative subject, they swallow hard and walk away. They must always be in control of themselves; they never can let their deepest reactions show. When they are bothered by something in their partners, they pretend not to notice. They have trained themselves not to be emotionally in-volved.

After years of practice, things are quite peaceful for the couple with the "safe relationship." They seldom argue. If one or the other experiences some depression, due to the continual suppres-sion of emotions . . . well, that's preferable to having to look at

61

the ugly worms that might appear if they started being candid.

Yes, they have a calm marriage—maybe even a "good" one, on the surface. But underneath, certain areas never are explored. No little honest worms are allowed to eat their way through the soil, loosening it and giving space for the roots to grow. This marriage is very free from risk—but it's not really alive anymore.

The alternative to the "safe relationship" is "no-barriers communication." In this chapter you will have a chance to examine the quality of your own communication together, and to work through some techniques of talking and listening, which Donna and I have found helpful.

Communication

NO BARRIERS = SHARING YOUR HEART

The following chart, adapted from the Family Life Conference Notebook,[1] illustrates five levels of communication:

Communication Levels	Meaning	Degree of Transparency	Number of People
1. Cliche'	Non-sharing		
2. Fact	Sharing what you know		
3. Opinion	Sharing what you think		
4. Emotion	Sharing what you feel		
5. No Barriers	Sharing your heart as a way of life		

1. *Cliché communication* allows one to remain safely isolated and alone. It is restricted to greetings and comments that express no opinions, feelings or real information. ("Hi, how are you?" "Fine, thank you.")
2. *Fact communication* consists only of the objective discussion of facts, gossiping or data analysis. It holds others at arm's length. ("Last night the weatherman said we'd have more rain today.")
3. *Opinion communication* involves sharing ideas and opinions that will open up a person as he expresses what he really thinks. ("I am really getting concerned about the garbage put out on television, and what it's doing to young people's minds.")
4. *Emotional communication* means sharing feelings and emotions leading to true communication, conveying one's hopes,

fears, likes, dislikes, aspirations, disappointments, joys, sorrows, needs, dreams, failures, desires, stresses, sources of fulfillment, discouragements and burdens. ("I got passed over again for promotion. I have to admit, getting that higher position meant a lot to me. I'm discouraged with this job.")

5. *No-barriers communication* is complete emotional and personal truthfulness. It is sharing your heart as a way of life. ("I'm tired this week, so I guess I'm more sensitive. When you made that comment about my housekeeping, I felt hurt and angry.")

As indicated on the chart, as the depth and breadth of communication increases, the number of people decreases. We will have no-barriers communication with very few people in our lives, but one of those certainly should be our mate!

No-barriers communication does *not* mean:
— psychological nakedness (sharing everything about anything with everyone) nor
— verbal impulsiveness (saying what you feel whenever you feel like it).

I've never told my wife some things about me, such as the details of how I kicked up my heels during my early college years. Nor does she care to know those secrets! Edith Schaeffer in *What is a Family* speaks of that certain thing you know you must never say to someone you love. Certain citadels should remain locked, private. But in a growing Christian marriage, these should be few.

I'm afraid that in many marriages, however, communication doesn't go beyond level three (sharing opinions). This can hardly be what the Author of marriage had in mind. Rather, I believe that the Lord wants us to learn no-barriers communication with our mates, difficult though that is. Just as He is delighted when we share our hearts with Him, He rejoices to see us being vulnerable with our earthly mates.

As you and your spouse interact on the following questions, be sure to use your looseleaf retreat Talkbook to record ideas.

Let's Begin Talking . . .

 Interaction

Each take a blank sheet from the Talkbook. Based on the above chart, choose the word or phrase that most accurately completes the following statements and write it on your paper, then share your answers with each other.

1. *I feel that most of the time our communication level is*
    cliché
    fact
    opinion
    emotion
    no barriers

Communication

2. *I feel that you communicate with me on the emotional level, conveying your hopes, fears, aspirations, failures, dreams and discouragements,*
    often
    sometimes
    seldom
    never

3. *I feel a need for more frequent communication on the emotion level . . .*
    yes
    no

4. *I feel that I know the real you*
    very well
    fairly well
    somewhat
    a little bit
    hardly at all

5. *I feel you know the real me*
    very well
    fairly well
    somewhat
    a little bit
    hardly at all

 Bible Study

1. Read aloud Genesis 2:24,25. What clue does this give about

the level of communication God intended for married couples?

2. Read Genesis 3:8-10. What emotion mentioned in verse 10 caused Adam to hide his nakedness? Fear also causes some mates to "hide from" each other, instead of risking open communication. What might such mates fear?

 ## Interaction

Remove two blank sheets from your Talkbook. Each take two minutes to write your answers for each question. Then share and discuss.

1. *Do I think that if I really opened up to you, you would make fun of me, criticize me or subtly reject me?* (Choose one answer.)

> *Yes, I think that would happen.*
> *Sometimes, I feel that way.*
> *No, I do not have that fear.*

2. *For me, the hardest thing about sharing my feelings is . . .*

Listening Exercise

Each partner should participate in turn. Discuss aloud, until each is satisfied that the other understands the feeling expressed.

Partner A: *A feeling I have been wanting to express to you is . . .*

Partner B: *What I hear you saying is* (express it back in different words) . . .

Partner A: *What I really mean is* (amplify on original feeling) . . .

 ## Affirmation

It is not always easy for me to share my feelings. But I really need you, and I want us to have the closeness that comes when we are vulnerable with each other. It encourages me to be open with you when you . . .

Prayer

Lord, You have shared Your heart so openly in Your Word. Help us learn to be open with You, and with each other. As we continue talking, show us any bad habits of communication that need to change. We cannot change ourselves; by Your Spirit, give us the power to be what You want us to be . . .

ADD EQUAL PARTS TRUTH AND LOVE

Communication

Many Christian couples would love to experience no-barriers communication. This is difficult, however, if bad habits have built up over the years. For example, a wife feels called to whip hubbie into shape with continual exhortations, like a cowpuncher herding reluctant cattle. If he does dare to admit a failure, she jumps in with, "Well, I've been trying to tell you that for years! What took you so long?"

Or a husband views himself as the strong silent type, who lives hard, but communicates mostly in grunts. *"Real* men don't share their deepest thoughts and feelings" seems to be his life motto.

Lest I be accused of stereotyping, let me say that in our marriage, I'm the talker. Not that I'm good at revealing deep feelings, but I'm usually the one with my mouth open. Recently Donna was relating an incident to some friends, and I interrupted her three times. After the third time she asked in exasperation, "Can I please finish just one sentence?"

"Sure," I agreed generously. "Which one would you like to finish?"

Most of us are not perfect communicators, but good communication is essential to marriage. In fact, what is marriage if not the disclosing of two people to each other on an ever-deepening level? Apart from this genuine interaction, marriage is merely a prison with walls fashioned by offspring and worldly possessions held in common.

In the first section of chapter 4, I discussed the basis of talking with each other honestly and without fear. Please take time now to read those pages aloud, if you have not done so.

Once you lay the initial foundation, certain listening and talking techniques may be helpful. Many excellent books on communication already exist; skim one of those listed in the bibliography before continuing further, if you sense many needs in this area. I'll give you only three brief guidelines, which have worked for Donna and me.

Waving the Red Flag

First of all, it's important to avoid certain "red-flag" words or phrases. Any of the following is guaranteed to raise your mate's hackles, and you'll probably be in for combat rather than a productive conversation:

1. "Always" ("You always forget to take out the garbage.")
2. "Never" ("You're never ready on time.")
3. "Why don't you ever . . ." ("Why don't you ever listen to me?")
4. "That figures!" (I.e., "I should have expected you'd do something dumb.")
5. "Never mind" ("You wouldn't understand anyway.")
6. "You're just like your mother!" (or father)
7. "Remember the time you . . ."

"I," not "You"

Second, as you express your feelings, avoid an accusing "you" message, as in "You make me angry," or "You're a lousy housekeeper." Instead, use an "I" message: "I am feeling very angry now," or "I feel frustrated when I come home to a messy house." It is not wrong to have feelings. What is wrong is either to repress them, pretending they don't exist, or to use them as sticks with which to beat one's mate over the head.

In *The Marriage Builder,* Lawrence J. Crabb, Jr. warns against communicating with the main goal of manipulating the partner to change. "But to be *primarily motivated* by the goal of winning a response from one's spouse that is designed to satisfy one's own desires...is a violation of love and therefore wrong. Love is essentially defined in terms of preoccupation with *other's* needs...Both partners must change their goals from manupulation to ministry. And the revolution requires supernatural intervention."[2]

The goal of your talking is not truth for manipulation, but truth for love's sake. "Speaking the truth *in love,*" as the apostle Paul said in Ephesians 4:15. Donna's reaction to my driving illustrates this. I have to admit, I sometimes drive too fast, often without realizing it. In the early days of our marriage, she would become more and more tense and finally burst out, "Slow down! You always drive too fast! You'll get us all killed!"

Even though I knew I was wrong, I didn't want to comply with my wife's tongue-lashings. I usually slowed down, but I was resentful, and I speeded up again before long.

Communication

When Donna learned the "I" message technique, she began to apply it here. Now she says something like, "I feel insecure when you drive so fast. Could you please slow down?" Instead of attacking me, she expresses a need, which I'm only too glad to help meet. Although I still forget sometimes, I believe my driving has improved since she's changed her tactics.

It's helpful if both partners can learn to analyze and express the reasons for their feelings. For example, Donna sometimes goes beyond stating "I feel insecure about your driving" and says something like, "I really care about you. I enjoy being married to you, and it scares me to think that I might lose you—or one of our children—through an accident." The more clearly she can paint the picture from her point of view, the more I understand that this is not an attack on me, but a legitimate fear.

My wife is a master of this art of intelligent explanation of her feelings. It's something she has learned. This takes practice, but it goes a long way toward resolving misunderstandings.

The "I" message is also useful in preventing outbursts of anger. Instead of indulging in the unhealthy extremes of suppression or explosion, mates can express anger honestly, yet calmly. "I am starting to get angry about this," my wife said when I was late for dinner several times in a row. She didn't nag or yell, which would have prompted me to put up my defenses. She simply expressed herself, and I got the message!

Chapter 8 deals with the topic of anger more fully in the section entitled "Fussin' and Forgiving." I also recommend H. Norman Wright's excellent book, *Communication: Key to Your Marriage*, which includes two chapters on anger.

Draw One Another Out

Third, and this is especially true if you're the family motor-mouth, learn to draw out your mate. Instead of the red-flag phrases, try some of these, and then keep your mouth firmly shut and your ears open.

1. *"Tell me how you feel about...." "What causes you to feel like that?"*
2. *"What have you been struggling with most this week (month)?" "How can I help you in this area?"*
3. *"Do you know that I love you? How can I be showing you this more clearly?"*
4. *"What has brought you the greatest joy in the past week (month)?"*

You cannot achieve openness overnight; learning to communicate is a lifelong process. Some couples might start by admitting one need or one genuine emotion. No matter what your starting point, as you prayerfully talk through the following questions, I think you'll be moving in a positive direction.

 Bible Study

Read aloud Ephesians 4:14-32. Brainstorm together and write down as many characteristics as possible of a good communicator, as seen in this passage.

 Interaction

Discuss the questions from each partner's point of view.

1. *Do I sometimes use faulty communication habits?* (Each should identify himself/herself on the following list, and explain why that description was chosen. Let the other then be content to respond with a knowing smile!)

    — *Gushy Gertie/Gordon*
    — *Sam/Samantha Strong-and-Silent*
    — *Nelda/Ned Know-it-all*
    — *Karl/Kari Kamakaze*
    — *Touchy Tom/Tina*
    — *Isabel/Ike Iceberg*
    — *Victor/Veronica Volcano*
    — *Paula/Peter Perfect*

2. *When I act like that, how does it make you feel?*

3. *I would be able to talk more calmly and openly with you if . . .*

4. *Do I sometimes use red-flag words? Which ones?*

5. *When bringing up negative things, do I sometimes attack with "you" statements, like "Your sloppy habits disgust me?" Give me some specific examples, and tell me how you'd rather hear them.*

6. *Drawing each other out takes time. Let's talk about when we could make this happen, perhaps on a weekly date. (Chapter 14 offers ideas for weekly talk times.)*

Communication

 Affirmation

Thank you for the ways in which you communicate well with me. I especially appreciate the way you . . .

 Prayer

Lord, again we are reminded of our human tendency to attack and accuse, when we need to accept and forgive. Let our heart's desire be to minister to each other, rather than to manipulate. Thank You for forgiving us completely, because of what Jesus did on the cross. Guide us in the coming months, so that we may see the barriers between us coming down . . . .

 Action Point

Let's review our discussion and set one simple goal. (For example: *We will establish a weekly talk time, beginning* _____ *at* _____ *o'clock.*) (Record your decision here and review it on your next retreat.)

Chapter 7
Mortar in Your Garden Wall

You have rolled up your sleeves and are well on your way to constructing a strong wall of defense for your marriage garden. Not any too soon, either, because here come the adversaries!

Just when it looks like you have thwarted enemy attack, WHOOSH! A mammoth gust of wind whirls by. If you're missing a vital ingredient, your beautiful wall becomes a heap of bricks!

What is that ingredient, the mortar, the glue that keeps the wall of a marriage garden from tumbling at the first gust of wind? That indispensible mortar is *spiritual oneness*.

The majority of lay couples whom we surveyed in preparation for this book checked "spiritual oneness" as a felt need in their relationships. What were they experiencing in their marriages that caused them to zero in on that phrase?

I believe they were saying, "I feel a need to be a more spiritual person, to have a closer walk with God, and my partner definitely would benefit from the same thing! If we were each drawing closer to Him, an atmosphere of spirituality would permeate our married life. This could be the secret to solving many of the problems that we experience in other areas as well."

Before we can talk about spiritual oneness, we must begin with *spiritual individuality*. Spiritual oneness is possible only if each partner in a marriage is spiritually alive. They both must have entered into personal relationships with God through Jesus Christ and be growing in their dependence on Him. It doesn't matter how far they've gotten in their spiritual pilgrimages, as long as they basically are moving forward.

With the above in mind, I'd like to offer a definition of *spiritual oneness*:

**Spiritual oneness is the harmonious unity of two grow-
ing Spirit-filled Christians in the close bond of marriage.**

When one or both partners is operating under the control of
self, rather than in obedience to God's Spirit, spiritual oneness
remains an impossible dream:

Oneness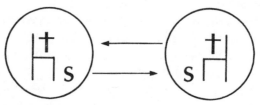

Partner A wants his/her
own way. Christ is
present in the life,
but is not at the controls.

Partner B is allowing
Christ to be on the
throne of the life,
with self dethroned.

This couple will not experience spiritual oneness until *both*
are allowing Christ to be on the throne of their lives, as in the
following:

An atmosphere of unity permeates this couple's relationship
because both are allowing the Holy Spirit to have the leadership
in their lives. (See the reprint of Bill Bright's booklet on the Spirit-
filled life, in appendix C.)

Naturally this does not mean that the second couple com-
prises two paragons of virtue who never argue and go around
constantly cooing at each other like lovesick canaries. They still
have stresses, problems and strong disagreements. In the midst
of attacks against their marriage, however, they can stand together
and fight the enemy, instead of fighting each other.

Who are the slithering enemies of your marriage? Their com-
mander-in-chief is Satan, who wants full control of planet Earth.
He certainly isn't happy when he finds two Spirit-filled individuals

whose marriage reflects the beautiful unity of Christ and the church (see Ephesians 5:22-33).

In *One Plus One* Tim Timmons writes, "Today the marriage relationship still exists to stand against the spiritual forces of evil. Satan's kingdom is defeated as husband and wife join in spiritual battle by depending together on the Lord. Therefore, Satan concentrates his major attacks on the marriage relationship because he knows that a couple living by God's principles is his greatest enemy."[1]

Who are the messengers of Satan, crawling toward your garden? They may take many forms:

- *trials, suffering* (causing discouragement or depression)
- *rejection* (by family or friends who do not understand your commitment to Christ)
- *economic pressure* (decreasing income, unemployment) - *feelings of isolation* (no close fellowship with other Christians)
- *sexual temptation* (thoughts, desires to find physical and emotional gratification outside of marriage)
- *"the blahs"* (getting in a rut that slowly is becoming a grave)
- *other enemies* (I'm sure you know of others)

Which of these is attacking *your* garden? The purpose of this chapter—and indeed, this book—is not to give you a stick with which to whap the little pests over the head. If you kill some, others will take their place. Rather, the purpose is to help you build a sturdy defense wall, *uniting* the two of you, while *protecting* against enemy advances.

Remember the garden scene in Genesis 3? The serpent cleverly waited until Eve was alone before he began his attack. His method hasn't changed: divide and conquer.

Therefore, both partners must be strong, as well as strongly united. They must be walking individually with God before they can experience spiritual oneness. If one partner is depending on the other for spiritual food, they both will find that frustration and disappointment are waiting just around the corner. When each is separately learning to know God better, however, their spiritual interaction can catalyze growth individually, and as a couple. In light of this, Christian mates should ask, "How can we best *encourage* each other in our daily relationships with the Lord?" In the workbook section we'll talk through this and discover some techniques for developing spiritual oneness.

Let's Begin Talking . . .

Oneness

 Interaction

Each take a sheet from the Talkbook. Working individually, draw a line graph of your personal spiritual pilgrimage from the beginning of your life to the present. Highs on the graph would represent times when you felt especially close to God, and so on. Then share and explain your graphs to each other.

> See to it, brothers, that none of you has a sinful, unbelieving heart that turns away from the living God. But encourage one another daily (Hebrews 3: 12,13).

How can Christian mates "encourage one another daily"? At Pentecost, after receiving the Holy Spirit, Peter preached a fiery message and about three thousand were added in one day to the small number of believers. In Acts 2:42, we read that these new (and old) converts devoted themselves to four things:
1. to the apostles' teaching
2. to the fellowship
3. to the breaking of bread
4. to prayer

Let's see how each of these relate to what you can do together, as a couple, to fan the flame of your lives with God. We will discuss them in the following order: (Points two and three from the above list have been condensed into one topic.)

Prayer (#4 above)—DEVOTED TO PRAYER
Communication and fellowship (#2 and 3)—WHERE IS YOUR FELLOWSHIP?
God's Word (#1)—GETTING GOD'S WORD INTO YOU

DEVOTED TO PRAYER

Rejoicing With Psalms

 Bible Study

Read aloud Philippians 4:4-7. With what exhortation does this passage begin?

One way to rejoice in the Lord while praying is to pray through a psalm, reading it aloud as a prayer to God and then adding personal "footnotes." Partners can alternate praying.

Oneness

 Interaction

Take Psalm 145 or a favorite psalm largely devoted to praise; use it as a guideline to rejoice in the Lord and worship Him. (Follow the example outlined below or invent a method that is meaningful to you.)

The **husband** reads Psalm. 145:1,2:

"I will exalt You, my God the King; I will praise Your name for ever and ever. Every day I will praise You and extol Your name for ever and ever."

He adds his own prayer:
Lord, I do exalt You. I am so awed by You; You are the King over the whole universe, and also over our marriage, over each of our lives. I truly want to remember to stop each day and praise Your name and lift You up because of who You are. . .

The **wife** reads Psalm 145:3,4:

"Great is the Lord and most worthy of praise; His greatness no one can fathom. One generation will commend Your works to another; they will tell of Your mighty acts."

She adds her own prayer:
Lord, when I think of Your greatness, I am overwhelmed. It's like a mountain I can't see to the top of. Father, we want to be talking about You to our children continually, so that they might be able to pass on to others all that You have done . . .

Continue throughout the Psalm.

Bible Study

Look again at Philippians 4:4,7. According to verse 6, prayer is the antidote for . . .

What does prayer result in (verse 7)? For how many things are we to pray?

Oneness

One of the many means of taking your requests to God is *conversational prayer*. It involves speaking brief sentence prayers back and forth on a particular topic, exhausting that topic before moving on to another. For example:

Husband: "Lord, I want to bring before You that meeting at the office tomorrow. You know how much I want that contract. Help me to leave it in Your hands."

Wife: "I agree, Lord. Give Jim real peace and confidence as he goes into the meeting. Remind him that You're there with him . . ." (and so on).

Interaction

Take some time to pray conversationally. Remember, it's not a monologue, but a three-way conversation between you, your partner and the Lord of Hosts. Listen to each other and don't be afraid to sit silently together and listen for the quiet voice of God.

Establish a Time

Bible Study

In Acts 2:42, the word prayer is plural in the original Greek. This verse and Acts 3:1 suggests that believers attended regular times of prayer in the temple. What is the value of having prayer at a specific time every day?

Interaction

No matter how many techniques for praying we have mastered, they will be useless if we do not find a time to pray. Can we establish a regular time for 15 to 30 minutes or so together with the Lord each day? (This should never be a substitute for individual quiet times.) Record your best ideas in the Talkbook.

Some suggestions:
- before breakfast
- after breakfast
- after supper
- after the kids are down
- as you jog together
- before lights-out

Affirmation

As I see the Holy Spirit at work in your prayer life, I especially am encouraged by . . .

Prayer

Father, we are learners in the school of prayer. On that basis we come to You with open hands. Lord, teach us to pray together! By Your grace, let our home become a house of prayer . . .

WHERE IS YOUR FELLOWSHIP?

Can't you just picture it? Jerusalem, July A.D. 33. The new church has more than three thousand members, divided up into neighborhood house groups. Overheard on a certain street one evening:

"Dad, why do we have to go to the house where Peter preaches—you know how long-winded he is!"

"Now son, let's not be critical."

"Oh, Daddy, Benjie's right! If we walked only three blocks further, we could get to John's house! He always finishes on time, and Mary makes the most delicious refreshments...."

Well, I don't know if it happened, but I wouldn't be surprised. It's always an important question for Christians: What part of Christ's body will I join? What are the criteria: nearness, warmth, preaching, greatest need?

What is a fellowship?

The early church had it easy, in some respects. Their fellowships were limited by the size of their houses! Today in America, many churches have thousands on their membership rolls. How can a Christian couple relate to several thousand other people?

Obviously, it can't be done! That's why it's essential to find one small "cell" within such a large body, one mini-fellowship to which we give our allegiance. Worship with the whole church is also vital, but only in a smaller unit will we experience deep unity and commitment to one another.

Oneness

Some possible fellowships within the larger church body are:
- prayer groups
- home Bible studies
- Sunday school classes
- outreach teams

To qualify, such a group must be small—probably twenty members at the most—and have as part of its goal bearing one another's burdens and encouraging each other to greater maturity in Christ.

 Bible Study

Read Ephesians 1:7 and 1 Corinthians 12:13. What two qualities do the people in a true Christian fellowship have in common? If you take part in such a group, in what ways might you be more free than when in an ordinary group of people? Record the insights in your Talkbook.

Review Acts 2:42, and add to your Talkbook the four foundational ""pillars" of the early church.

As you read over what you've just written in your Talkbook, perhaps you'll get a feel for the kind of fellowship within the church body to which you want to attach yourselves.

As a general rule, it isn't a good idea to choose a fellowship —or a church, either—simply because it "needs you." Of course, you will want to serve and use your spiritual gifts wherever you are, but if the group is in really bad shape, it's more likely that your own growth will be stifled.

Carefully choose your church and your fellowship—then give

them your commitment. That doesn't mean be at the church every time the janitor flips on the lights, but do find your niche there and wholeheartedly serve within it. Don't be part of the herd of "Church-hoppers," who are doomed to wander forever in a continuous quest, coming to rest only briefly before casting off in their endless search for the perfect church. (If they ever find it and join, it won't stay perfect long!)

In Acts 2:47 we read: "The Lord added to their number daily those who were being saved." Why? It was because not only were these new believers witnessing to everything that moved, but they also were practicing loving one another. The world saw a group of people experienced in the art of loving, and it looked pretty inviting. That's part of what life lived in commitment to a smaller fellowship of believers does for us.

Oneness

 Interaction

Discuss your commitment to a fellowship of believers. First, each take time separately to write a few sentences in answer to the questions:

1. *To what kind of fellowship would I like to belong?*
2. *What do I picture in my mind as the ideal for our involvement in such a fellowship? (I.e., roles we would play, time involved, level of commitment to the other members, etc.)*

Now share and discuss the answers.

We will take the following action toward becoming part of a fellowship: (Record answer in your Talkbook.)
What changes might we want to make, either in our place of worship, or else in our level of involvement where we are? (Record ideas in your Talkbook.)

 Affirmation

Husband and wife each affirm the other with:
You seem to be able to serve the body of Christ in the areas of . . .
(Consult the bibliography for books that aid in discerning your own spiritual gifts.)

Prayer

Father, guide us as we seek to serve and love our particular part of the body of Christ. If we need to make changes, impress these in our hearts by Your Spirit.

GETTING GOD'S WORD INTO YOU

Oneness

It's important to "get into the Word of God," as the saying goes. Even more so is "getting God's Word into you"!

One excellent way to do this is to interact with your mate regularly on passages of Scripture. This involves something a little more thorough than mumbling "Great sermon, wasn't it!" over mouthfuls of Sunday dinner. On the other hand, it doesn't need to be deep, intensive study; you might prefer to do that alone. (See the bibliography for suggested books on personal quiet times.) You can incorporate this into the time you've set aside for prayer, or pick another regular time.

Trading insights on a passage of Scripture is a great means of keeping your spiritual juices flowing. The Dead Sea illustrates this principle—it's dead because water flows only *in*, not *out*. If we take God's Word, but never give any of it back *out*, we're in for a severe case of spiritual constipation!

 Bible Study

The following is a sample method of reading the Bible together, which could be used in your devotional times.

Each read aloud 1 Corinthians 13:1-8, from two different versions. Then, each read the passage silently several times, making notes of insights. Next, share your observations with each other. (It's helpful to keep a Bible handbook or commentary nearby, to answer thorny questions.) Then, each attempt to answer:

What does the passage mean to me personally?
What might the Lord be saying to me through it right now?

There are many methods of meeting together over God's Word, besides the one mentioned above. For example:

— Use a daily devotional book, and discuss the Scripture indicated.
— Attend a Bible study together.
— Take notes in church and discuss them afterwards.
— Have a weekly "tape night," on which you listen to and discuss a cassette Bible message.
— Share insights with each other from your daily quiet times.
(This might motivate you to have them more consistently!)

 ## Interaction

What is the best way for us to interact together over God's Word? What specific time slot will we find in our schedule?

 ## Affirmation

"And I am sure that God who began the good work within you will keep right on helping you grow in His grace until His task within you is finally finished on that day when Jesus Christ returns"(Philippians 1:6).

 ## Prayer

Father, we realize that our marriage must take second place to the relationship each of us has with You. Help us grow closer and closer to You; let your Holy Spirit have His way in our lives, that Christ might be lifted up in and through us. We want to see in our marriage a oneness that only You can bring . . .

 ## Action Point

Let's review our discussion and set one simple goal. (For example: We will begin a regular time of interacting in Bible reading and prayer, every _____ at _____.)
(Record this decision here and review it at your next retreat.)

Chapter 8

"You Get the Shovel, I'll Take the Rake"

Understanding

A famous biologist was asked what he would conclude about God, the Creator, based on his years of scientific study. "An inordinate fondness for beetles," he replied immediately, because he was struck with the variety and beauty of the some 220,000 species of beetle that have been classified so far.

If he'd looked at mankind in the same light, this scientist might have concluded that God had "an inordinate fondness for people"! The barest scratch on the surface of even the smallest number of human beings will reveal the most amazing differences.

Whether these dissimilarities are rooted in racial, cultural, religious, sexual, educational or economic grounds, the fact is that no two people on earth are exactly alike. And the more different any two are, the more likely that misunderstanding, distrust or downright dislike will spring up between them.

How can two partners, who set out jointly to cultivate their marriage garden, enrich the soil with their individual uniquenesses? How can they help their differences become, not a gulf between them but a glue that bonds them together?

This chapter will help you answer these questions as you explore together the following areas:

DOES DIFFERENT EQUAL WRONG?
   How are we different and similar, and how do we handle the tensions that result?
WHO'S IN CHARGE HERE?
   Who is in charge of what in our home?
FUSSIN' AND FORGIVING.
   How can we fight and yet forgive?

The goal is that, through the interaction, you will deepen your appreciation and acceptance of each other—faults and all. I trust that you also will come up with some practical ideas with which to grease any wheels of your relationship that are squeaking from friction!

Remember, the Bible study is just as important as the interaction. Take notes in your loose-leaf Talkbook.

Understanding

Let's Begin Talking ...

 Interaction

Each take a separate sheet of paper and make two headings, one for each of you. Skim these lists of opposites and write down the ones which tend to describe you. Then write the ones which tend to describe your mate. Now compare notes. You each may learn some new things about yourself from the way your mate sees you!

Who am I? Who is My Mate?

Either this:	Or this:
outgoing	quiet
quick-thinker	slow-to-decide
city type	country lover
humorous	serious
stern	gentle
leader	reluctant leader
punctual	often late
night owl	early bird
perfectionist	hang-loose
impulsive	disciplined
people-centered	project-centered
party-goer	stay-at-home
needs a crowd	needs time alone
organizer	let-it-happen
practical	idea person
optimistic	pessimistic
strong-willed	yielding
easy-going	temperamental
self-confident	hesitant

DOES DIFFERENT EQUAL WRONG?

I am special/you are special

 Bible Study

Read Psalm 139 aloud to each other, alternating verses. Then go back through and write down in your Talkbook five ways in which the Lord is intimately acquainted with you. Make it specific to your own life. For example, for verse three, "You discern my going out," a wife might say, "You know each time I go to the supermarket." Then discuss:

Understanding

1. *Is God taken by surprise at the way our lives are unfolding? (See vv. 15,16.)*

2. *How much are we on God's mind? (See vv. 17,18.)*

3. Read aloud Matthew 6:25-34. *To what two things in nature does Jesus compare people? What is He trying to tell us about how God views us?*

FOOD FOR THOUGHT: *If people in general are very special to God, then I am very special to Him and my mate is equally special to Him. Are there ways in which we are not living as if this is true?*

 Interaction

Look again at the descriptive words you chose for each other from the list on the previous page. Now transfer your selections back to the list in the book this way: First, come to a general agreement as to which words tend to describe each of you. Then identify yourselves by marking the terms that describe you. The wife should draw a circle around her words and the husband draw a box around his, even if they are the same.

Example:

organizer	let-it-happen
practical	idea person
optimistic	pessimistic
strong-willed	yielding
easy-going	temperamental

For each set of opposites (circle around one word, box around the word across from it), ask each other:

How are our differences in this area causing tensions in our marriage? (Be specific.)

What can we do to help relieve this tension? (List your answers in your retreat Talkbook.)

Understanding

For example, I am your basic good-time Charlie. (I put a box around humorous), while Donna is much more serious (she circled that word). I tend to try to make her laugh when she's telling me about a problem that seems quite weighty to her. We have learned to relieve this tension, however, in two ways. First, I have resolved to listen to her when she's upset, without trying to crack a joke. Second, if I sense she's becoming a Pitiful Pearl, then I have advance permission to gently inject a little humor.

Go through the lists again, this time noting which words have both a box and a circle around them. Ask:

Are our similarities causing tension?

How might we resolve this?

Write down specific ideas in your Talkbook.

Donna and I are extreme opposites in many ways, except one: We both tend to be undisciplined in aspects of our personal lives. This has caused more problems than any of our differences. For example, when the alarm clock would go off, we each expected the other to bound out of bed to get things going. After sleeping through the alarm several times, we had to come up with a solution. Now when the alarm sounds, Donna wakes up enough to give me several swift kicks, after which I am alert enough to get up and make the coffee. Even after several years of marriage, we often need to talk through ways we can prod each other into greater self-discipline.

Picking Each Other Up

 Bible Study

Read Ecclesiastes 4:9-12. List in your Talkbook the five reasons why "two are better than one."

How could we elaborate on or add to these from our own experience?

 Interaction

Discuss together and write down:

1. *What seem to be each of our strong points? Weak areas?*

2. *What area of strength would I like to develop even further? Some ideas on how this might happen . . .*

3. *What area of weakness would I like to see strengthened? Some ideas on how . . .*

As you share ideas, remember why "two are better than one"! Don't forget to include suggestions for how you can help your partner develop a strength or bolster a weakness. For example, a husband might offer to take over part of the household responsibilities, to give his wife more time and energy to develop a creative interest. A wife might agree to embark on an exercise program with her husband, because she knows he needs the motivation of having a fellow-sufferer.

"It should, however, be borne in mind that no amount of self-improvement or self-effort can bring any of these traits into our lives without the power of the Holy Spirit," Tim LaHaye writes in *Spirit-Controlled Temperament*. "From this we conclude that the most important single thing in the life of any Christian is to be filled with the Holy Spirit."[1] (I recommend Dr. LaHaye's books, which provide a careful analysis of four basic temperament types coupled with thorough descriptions of living in the power of the Holy Spirit.)

 Affirmation

You and I are two very different people. I am glad of that; our lives would be so unbalanced and dull if we were just alike! I especially admire and appreciate in you the quality of . . .

 Prayer

Lord, we lay our many differences before You. You created each of us unique for a special purpose. And yet You say that we

also are to become as one! Lord, that kind of harmony in our marriage would be a miracle that could come only from You. Make it happen, we pray, by Your spirit. We place our lives into Your hands. . .

WHO'S IN CHARGE HERE?

Understanding

Throwing out that question today is like tossing a bucket of warm mash into a pen with a hundred hungry pigs. It's easy to get trampled to death in the wild stampede of opinions that ensue!

In answering that question for yourselves, I encourage you to examine God's Word. I'll tell you what Donna and I feel is right for us, and we also recommend several excellent books in the bibliography (some of which disagree over the question of authority in the home). Most important however, is that you two agree on who will be the boss of what in your own home!

 Bible Study

Read Ephesians 5:21-33.

If both of us are believers in Christ, then we both are members of Christ's body. If this is true, then who truly is the "head of the household" at our home? What are the implications for us, if Christ is the head of our home? (Record answers in your Talkbook.)

What instructions are given to the husband? (vv. 25-30,33)

What instructions are given to the wife? (vv. 22,24,33)

I believe that in deciding who is in charge of what in the home, there is a wide scope of what is acceptable and pleasing to God. When Donna and I first married, we tended to operate under the view that I should make all of the major decisions and many of the minor ones in my position as "head" of my wife. Of course, I usually consulted Donna first and often changed course after her input, but I still considered myself basically "in charge."

Yet, we really were not happy with this. For one thing, I am extremely busy. I was spending a lot of time making decisions that Donna could have made for me. Also, I often travel, and life can't be suspended until I return. Donna was becoming frustrated; she was quite willing to make decisions in certain areas, but our division of labor did not allow her to do so.

Gradually my eyes have been opened to see my wife's

capabilities, and we have expanded her base of authority. We have a more equal partnership now, with each of us taking responsibilities in certain areas, and each consulting with the other before taking action on major issues.

For example, Donna is the main decision-maker in decorating our home, thinking through the development of our children and entertaining. I oversee areas such as major purchases, bookkeeping and correspondence. Different couples might assign these differently, according to their particular strengths.

 ## Interaction

What about us? Let's discuss who should be the main decision-maker for each area of home and family responsibility. (Remember that the one in charge should get the partner's input before making major decisions.)

Which areas do we prefer to handle jointly? (Add your own to the list below.)

1. Overall finances (saving, insurance, major purchases, etc.)
2. Bookkeeping (checkbook, etc.)
3. Children's development (Both will share in carrying out, but probably one will be the main planner.)
4. Interior decoration
5. Lawn and garden
6. Auto upkeep
7. Division of household tasks
8. Division of tasks related to children
9. Entertaining and hospitality
10. Correspondence (to relatives, etc.)

What if one gives input and the other doesn't agree? If you've decided ahead of time who will oversee what, stick to it as much as possible. If a major disagreement bubbles up and can't be resolved after prayer and discussion, however, then God's Word seems to indicate that the man makes the final choice and takes responsibility for the results. The wife yields, even while admitting she doesn't agree, and she lets him live with the consequences of the decision, good or bad.

If the wife is lifting up her husband with genuine respect, and the husband is honoring her with deep love, as seen in the

Ephesians 5 passage, then many of the difficulties over "who's in charge" will fade into the background.

 Bible Study

Read Ephesians 5:21 again.

How can we apply that Scripture when we disagree on a decision? Upon what is our submission to each other based? (Read aloud Philippians 2:5-8.)

Understanding

Unwillingness to give in, at least some of the time, to my mate's wishes, might mean I need to ask myself, "Who's in charge of my life right now? Who is in the driver's seat? Am I, or is the Holy Spirit?"

I can put on the brakes the moment I realize that self and selfish motives have taken over my heart again. Then I simply tell God that I agree with Him that this is wrong (i.e., I confess my sins). I ask Him to fill me again with His Spirit, and I thank Him for doing so. (Review the Holy Spirit section in chapter 3. See also appendix C, especially "Spiritual Breathing.")

 Interaction

"The one who submits in a given issue is the stronger one in that situation." Discuss this statement, thinking about the ways in which Christ was submissive.

Is there a facet of our lives in which you would like to become the decision-maker? Is there an area of your decision-making which you'd rather deed over to me?

Interior decoration is kind of a hobby of mine. I'd love to be the one to decide how our home looks! Yet, Donna also has strong artistic tendencies, so this was the area of greatest conflict early in our marriage. Now I see that Donna's well-being is affected by her having the main input regarding decorating our home. She sees our home as a physical extension of her personality and views my domination there as a threat to her womanhood. So I submit to her in this area, out of love for her. She graciously accepts my suggestions, but is free not to act on them.

Affirmation

I respect you for having more experience and interest than I in the areas of . . .

I affirm your right to take the major responsibility over these, and I trust your capability in handling them. I stand ready to offer ideas and assistance, as you call on me.

 Prayer

Lord, we admit that we sometimes have been more interested in getting our own way than in letting You have Your way with us. Draw us closer to Yourself. Fill us anew with Your Spirit, that we might have the strength to yield to one another out of the overflow of our relationship with You . . .

FUSSIN' AND FORGIVING

A well-known women's Bible teacher in Houston encourages all married couples to engage in what she calls "fussin'." Couples have to fuss, she claims, to air their differences. If they aren't fussin' they aren't communicating honestly!

She's right; mates who have absolutely no outward disagreements probably have chosen the alternative: the safe-but-dead relationship. Yet the opposite is even more unpleasant—the two who use every minor difference as an excuse to start World War III. How do we find the balance? And, once we've fussed, how do we forgive and begin afresh?

First the Fussin'

 Bible Study

Read Ephesians 4:15.
What is the "check" we should put upon speaking the truth? As we lovingly speak the truth, what will result?

Read Ephesians 4:26-27.
What would be considered "sinful anger?" If we allow this to happen, what can occur?

Although we are told in Ephesians 4:31 to "get rid of...anger,"

God does allow for our human tendency to get irritated, as seen in verse 26. This is especially true in the intimate closeness of a marriage. How do we deal with anger in a healing, Christ-honoring way?

Chuck Swindoll, in his book *Strike the Original Match*, lists the following seven rules for a good fight:[2]

Understanding

1. Be committed to honesty and mutual respect.
2. Make sure that the weapons are not deadly (such as explosions of temper, profanity, cutting remarks).
3. Agree that the time is right.
4. Be ready with a positive solution, soon after the swing.
5. Watch your words and guard your tone.
6. Don't swing at your mate in public.
7. When it's over, help clean up the mess. This involves kindness, tenderness and forgiveness.

I'd like to add an eighth, based on Ephesians 4:26: Don't sleep on it! Settle the issue before you settle down for the night. If you go to bed angry, a seed of bitterness can start to take root.

 Interaction

Which ones of these eight rules do we most often violate?

In what areas do we probably need to be more truthful with each other?

In what situations do we need to learn to express truth more lovingly?

Write down ideas. This would be a good time to review chapter 6, on no-barriers communications.

Don't Forget to Forgive

Someone has said, "To forgive is to set the prisoner free, only to discover that the prisoner was you." But what if we don't feel like forgiving, or think that we simply cannot? Some partners have cut each other deeply, until scar has built up over scar. What then? How do we bring God into the negative? Ney Bailey, popular speaker for Campus Crusade for Christ, recommends three steps:[3]

Step One: Giving Thanks

Bible Study

Read Ephesians 5:20 and 1 Thessalonians 5:18. Does it seem illogical to thank God for the faults and failures of our mates? If so, read Romans 8:28-29. God actually can use the failures of others to help make us more like Christ! When we thank God for what we don't like, we bring God into our "negative" circumstances and release His power to work.

Interaction

What particular negatives in our relationship do we need to thank God for?

Step Two: Blessing, Not Cursing

Bible Study

Read James 3:9-11. "Blessing" means "speaking well of"; "cursing" means "not speaking well of." According to verse 9, what is wrong with cursing other people? (This refers to not only what we say openly, but also what we say of them in our hearts.)

Interaction

Does it seem that we have inwardly or outwardly cursed one another lately? What have been the results?

Step Three: Seeing Our Forgiveness Clearly

Bible Study

Read Ephesians 4:32 and Colossians 3:12,13. On what basis are we asked to forgive others? (Pause for a time of silent reflection. Consider the many ways in which Christ has forgiven you. Ask Him to make His forgiving love real in your own heart, so that

Understanding

you can be reach out to your mate in forgiveness.)

 Affirmation

I accept you as given to me from God's hand. I am very grateful that you also accept and receive me, with all my faults. I want to begin truly "blessing" you in my heart, and not "cursing" you, as God enables me. I want to say that I forgive you for . . .

Do you forgive me for . . .

Understanding

 Prayer

Father, we often have broken the rules for a good fight and have hurt each other deeply. We each bear scars, and it's been hard to forgive. Lord, give us, by Your Spirit, a new ability to forgive and forget. Thank You for paying such an expensive price in order to be able to forgive us and to bring each of us into our own relationship with You . . .

 Action Point

Let's review our discussion and set one simple goal. (For example: *For the next thirty days we will each thank God in prayer for our understanding of the negatives in our relationship and for His forgiveness and for how He can work in those negatives to make us more like Christ.*)

(Record your goal here and review it during your next retreat.)

Chapter 9

Your Vines Intertwining

Intimacy

I enjoy confronting situations which are disorganized and creating efficient order out of the chaos. So one day, as I impatiently waited in line for some "fast food," watching personnel scurry to and fro with styrofoam boxes of hamburgers, I mentally streamlined their whole operation.

Nothing was wrong with that—it kept my mind occupied while I waited. But if I were to take that efficiency-expert tendency of mine home and use it in the bedroom—look out! I might logically, though selfishly, analyze our sexual relationship as follows: I have strong physical needs. How can we best organize our lives to fulfill these needs most quickly and completely?

Sorry, guys, that just won't cut it! God has designed women in an unbelievably complex way. As someone has said, "If you want to know what men are like, ask a woman. If you want to know what women are like, ask the Lord!"

Because men and women are so unique in how they approach sex, it's a wonder they manage to come together at all! It never would happen, apart from the strong sexual drive built into us by the Creator Himself.

Let's begin by looking at some of the male-female differences as they concern the sexual relationship. Then we'll see how these differences can unify through the concept of cultivating intimacy. Finally, we'll interact on specific questions about the physical union of a couple.

VIVE LA DIFFERENCE!

If we don't grasp that there are very real, God-given contrasts between how men and women view sex, we are doomed to

95

frustration and disappointment. Once we accept that major differences exist, however, we can begin to work with them constructively.

Consider the following chart, adapted from the Family Life Conference notebook:

DIFFERENCES IN SEXUALITY[1]

Intimacy

	MEN	WOMEN
VIEW OF SEX	Physical Compartmentalized Physical oneness Variety Sex is high priority	Relational Holistic Emotional oneness Security Other priorities may be higher
STIMULATED BY	Sight Smell	Touch Attitudes Actions Words
NEEDS	Respect Admiration Physically needed Not to be put down	Understanding Love Emotionally needed Time
SEXUAL RESPONSE	Not cyclical Quick excitement Initiates (usually) Difficult to distract	Cyclical Slow excitement Responder (usually) Easily distracted

Let's Begin Talking . . .

 Interaction

Each take a sheet of paper from your Talkbook. Working separately, answer the following:

Based on this chart, where do we see our male-female differences causing points of tension? (Share your answers, but do not attempt to find solutions at this point.)

For a man, sexual union involves a specific action, measurable in terms of "how many times a week." He subconsciously uses sex as a repository, a place to release all of his built-up fears, joys, tensions and excitements. Along with that, he accomplishes a literal physical release of built-up fluid. His need for this release

96

is extremely strong. Failure to "perform" sexually devastates his ego.

For a woman, sexual intercourse is the culmination of her responses to tenderness, sacrificial love and even spiritual leadership from her husband. She views it much less as a specific act, and more as a part of the whole atmosphere in which she, as a married woman, moves. The act is like the frosting on the cake, and the cake must first be baked, before it can be frosted!

"Men use intimacy to get sex. Women use sex to get intimacy," commented a journalist quoted in *Time Magazine*.[2]

I strongly believe that much sexual dissatisfaction in marriage springs from different approaches to sex by the two partners.

Intimacy

INTIMACY: BAKING YOUR CAKE

Dr. James Dobson describes this dilemma in his excellent book, *What Wives Wish Their Husbands Knew About Women*:

> How can this sexual distinction interfere with a marital relationship where genuine love is evident? Simply this: unless a woman feels a certain closeness to her husband at a particular time—unless she believes he respects her as a person—she may be unable to enjoy a sexual encounter with him. A man can come home from work in a bad mood, spend the evening slaving over his desk or in his garage, watch the eleven o'clock news in silence, and finally hop into bed for a brief nighttime romp. The fact that he and his wife have had no tender moments in the entire evening does not inhibit his sexual desire significantly. He sees her on her way to bed in her clingy nightgown and that is enough to throw his switch. But his wife is not so easily moved. She waited for him all day, and when he came home and hardly even greeted her, she felt disappointment and rejection. His continuing coolness and self-preoccupation put a padlock on her desires; therefore, she may find it impossible to respond to him later in the evening. Let me go one step further: when a woman makes love in the absence of romantic closeness, she feels like a prostitute.[3]

She feels like a prostitute! What's a poor guy to do?

 Bible Study

Read aloud Ephesians 5:33a and 1 Peter 3:7. What will

97

happen if a husband is not considerate or understanding with his wife (1 Peter 3:7b)? The next section will show how you might apply these verses to your marriage.

Dobson says that a wife must sense a "certain closeness" to her husband; otherwise, she will feel used in the sexual union. This certain closeness, or *intimacy*, is absolutely vital to the marital happiness of a wife, and especially to her ability to yield herself joyfully in the sexual union with her husband.

Intimacy

SEVEN SECRETS OF INTIMACY

Let's define the somewhat nebulous term "intimacy" by discussing several factors that can contribute to it. Under each point I will list a couple of things Donna and I have done. Then you can think up what might work for you!

A WORD TO HUSBANDS: Cultivating a sense of intimacy cannot be reduced to a formula. No single thing or set of things that I do causes my wife to feel close or intimate with me. Rather, an atmosphere of caring love permeates (or should!) our whole relationship. I am learning a thousand different ways to act out "I love you," so that she hears it at every level of her being.
The secrets of intimacy can be *learned*. I know, because I have had to learn them myself. By nature, I'm your basic insensitive clod. I do not have some sixth sense or intuition that tunes me in to a woman's needs. But over the years, as I have learned to depend on God's Spirit and as my wife has learned to communicate her needs, I have gained some insight. I am still learning, though!

A WORD TO WIVES: This section might look like a double-barreled shotgun aimed at your husband, but don't get trigger-happy! You have a choice: You can either criticize him for all the things he hasn't done, or praise him for what he has done to create a climate of intimacy for you. If you are now on a marriage retreat together, your man has made giant strides in the right direction! Don't blast him with his failures; instead, consider how you can gently encourage him with a few positive suggestions.

Husbands, here are seven ideas to get you started toward

the intimacy that your wife is just waiting for. If the two of you brain-storm, you probably will find seventy-seven others!

(During each Interaction phase record your ideas in your Talkbook.)

1. Be a Romeo.

Most women are incurable romantics. So you don't feel comfortable playing Romeo? Who cares! She'll be so appreciative, she won't care if you feel a little silly! Tell her you love her...call her from work just to say you miss her ...surprise her with flowers...leave passionate notes under her pillow...take her out to a movie and hold her hand...kidnap her and take her to a motel.... Any means by which you can inject a little romance into your daily lives will reap great rewards.

From us

—On one occasion I surprised Donna by giving her a piece of lingerie so exotic, she has to keep it hidden in a bottom drawer in a flame-retardant package!

— I tell my wife 867 times a day that I love her. She says that's just about the right frequency.

 Interaction

From you

(Husband:) *How could I more fully demonstrate romantic love? What says "I love you" most clearly to you?*
(Wife:) *How am I hindering you from being more of a Romeo (nagging, not building you up, etc.)?*

2. Get her out of her rut.

I trust that no husband thinks that the mother of his children has a soft job, staying home with the kids while he sword-fights his way through the daily combat at the office. If such a person does exist, I dearly hope his wife temporarily becomes incapacitated, so that he has to take over the home front for a week or so!

Mothers—especially mothers of preschoolers, of which we have two—desperately need some breathing space every week. If the mother also works full time outside the home, she's got a job description even Wonder Woman would be hard pressed to fill.

Uninterrupted contact with our two little ring-tailed tooters, over an extended period of time, has been known to produce symptoms of insanity in Donna. And we have a teenager, too. Donna needs some time to herself! This is not an "extra," but an absolute necessity.

Intimacy

From us

— We've found some dependable neighborhood teenagers, and have trained them to work well with our children. Now Donna usually can get a babysitter on short notice.

— I insist that my wife take all or part of one day off a week, and I pay for household help to enable her to do this.

— Every six months I whisk Donna away for a marriage retreat weekend!

 Interaction

From you

(Wife:) *These are some of my feelings about being cooped up with the kids all week (describe your feelings):*

(Husband): *How can I best help you escape from your rut at least once a week?*

3. Give high priority to a common interest.

A husband comes home drained from his day's work. He switches on the television and shifts his mind into neutral, giving relief from the high gear of the day. Or maybe he disappears into his workshop.

It isn't wrong for a husband to occasionally unwind in front of the television or with a hobby. However, if your unwinding consistently takes a couple of hours each evening, and does not include interaction with your wife or children, perhaps you should re-evaluate it.

You might substitute a common pursuit. Listen to a Christian message together, or to music...read aloud to each other...go to a concert...go for walks...take up square-dancing or ceramics.... Your imagination's the limit! Believe it or not, these common pursuits affect your wife's feelings of intimacy and therefore her sexual response.

From us
— We met veterinarian author James Herriot on a recent trip to England and have since spent some hilarious evenings reading aloud to each other from one of his books.
—We are trying very hard to go jogging together a few evenings a week. Because of our small children and my travel schedule, this one's still in the "pilot" stage.

 Interaction

From you
What one common interest could we develop? When and how would we pursue it?

4. Include her in your thinking and planning.

I'm definitely still working on this one. Just today, in fact, Donna got upset with me because I decided (based on logic practicality, of course) that I need to take a two-week transatlantic trip this spring. She would have greatly appreciated being in on the decision-making process, rather than being informed of it after the fact. (My defense, "But I haven't bought my ticket yet!" was admittedly shaky.)

Can you share with your wife a little more of what goes on at the office? Does she know what's on your mind regarding the future of your job...your relationship with the boss...your next vacation...the purchase of your next car?

From us
— I am learning to talk in more detail about what happens during my trips away from home. Donna is learning to draw me out with questions.

 Interaction

From you
(Husband:) *In which of the following areas would you prefer to be included more often in my thinking and planning?*
— details of my day at work

— my future
— purchases I am considering
— business trips
— family vacations
— relationships with relatives
— relationships with co-workers and friends

(Wife:) *Help me think of times and ways I could draw you out.*

Intimacy

5. Communicate acceptance of her.

Nothing is as likely to squelch a wife's sexual response as negative feelings about herself. And some of those negative feelings unwittingly are transmitted by us husbands. Unfortunately, a husband often doesn't connect his 6 o'clock question, "When was the last time this rug was vacuumed?" with his wife's 10 o'clock statement, "I just don't feel like it tonight."

Are you praising your wife's cooking…her housekeeping …her mothering of your children? Do you compliment her figure…her choice of clothes…her femininity? Do you tell her she is sexually attractive to you? This becomes more important to her with each passing year!

From us
— I am learning to reduce greatly the number of "constructive" comments I make about Donna's cooking.
— I frequently tell her how attractive she is to me.

 Interaction

From you
(Husband:) *Do you sense a critical spirit from me in any area? Right now, in what areas of your life do you feel the need for me to communicate acceptance?*

6. Take spiritual initiative.

After several years of ministering to Christian couples, I feel that this is one of the areas of greatest disappointment for the Christian wife: Her husband just isn't the "spiritual leader" she thought she was marrying.

When we men hear that term "spiritual leader," we tend

to get a cold knot in the bottom of the stomach. Whatever that means, I know I'm not it! To be a "spiritual leader," I need to have the faith of George Mueller, the charisma of Billy Graham and the teaching ability of Chuck Swindoll, right?

Wrong. Look again at the heading: *Take spiritual initiative.* That's what our wives would like to see more of—their *husbands* sometimes being the one to suggest, for example, "Let's read the Bible together," for example, or "Why don't we stop and pray about this?" (This subject is pursued in more detail in chapter 7.)

Do you believe that your wife will be more likely to respond to you sexually if you take more spiritual initiative? It's true!

From us
— I often initiate a brief prayer time just before lights-out, in which we commit to the Lord the needs and problems of that day.
— I am trying to remember to read aloud from the *Living Light* (a devotional book that is pure Scripture) after supper while the family is still at the table.

 ## Interaction

From You
(Husband:) *Let's talk about ways in which I could take more initiative spiritually. (*Note: It's better to have one good idea and carry it through, than to have ten and be unable to implement them.) *Will you gently remind me when I forget to carry out what we've planned?*

7. Set the stage.
Whereas a husband can be ready to leap into bed at a moment's notice, wives need more time to prepare, mentally and emotionally, for intercourse. Dr. Dobson points out the homemaker's dilemma: "A loving wife who is diligently maintaining her home and caring for the needs of her family is unlikely to feel like a seductive mistress who tempts her husband into the bedroom."[4]

A husband can be a tremendous help by doing some

Intimacy

advance planning on a day in which he'd like to enjoy physical union with his wife. By pitching in and helping with the kids and supper dishes, he can give her a much-needed break, allowing her time to make the mental switch from laundress to lover. After the kids are in bed, instead of just hitting the sack, he can further prepare the setting with a relaxed time of tender communica tion. Remember from the previous chart that women are stimulated by *words*.

Along with this, I might mention the need for women to have regular physical examinations. Excessive tiredness could have causes other than the energy drain of mother-hood, great though that is. Husbands should urge their wives to get thorough checkups, including blood sugar tests.

From us

— On certain nights, I send Donna up to our room immediately after supper. I put the dishes and kids to rest, while she relaxes, reads, maybe takes a short nap.

— We have instituted what we call "tuddle times "—tuddle = talk + cuddle—times of tender communication, of unwinding and switching gears together.

 Interaction

From you

Let's brainstorm together on how we could better set the stage for our intimate times. Do we need to make changes in

    — the atmosphere of our bedroom?

    — our daily routine?

    — our routine on certain evenings?

 Affirmation

(Wife:) *I appreciate your seeking to understand me and my need for intimacy. I wnat to express my needs in an encouraging, helpful way.*

(Husband:) *I greatly value you as a woman. Your feminine sexuality is very attractive to me. I am trusting God to help me be more sensitive to express intimacy in ways that are meaningful to you.*

Prayer

(Husband's prayer:)

Lord, slow me down. My desires are sometimes so strong that I forget to be tender. Help me remember to create a climate of intimacy for my wife, that she might truly feel secure in my love....

BEING YOUR HUSBAND'S GREATEST FAN

It wouldn't be fair to get on the husband's case without mentioning the flip side. In her book *Creative Counterpart*, Linda Dillow refers to this as the wife being her hubby's "greatest fan." She says, "Psychiatrists say a man's most basic needs, apart from warm sexual love, are approval and admiration."[5]

 Bible Study

Read Ephesians 5:33b. The thesaurus lists the following words under "respect": *adore, esteem, honor, regard, revere, look up to.*

(Wife:) *How does this verse relate to "being my husband's greatest fan"? Have I truly respected him if I have not verbalized my respect?*

 Interaction

(Wife:) *Have I been running you down in any way, making you feel I don't respect you? In what specific areas would you especially like to hear me express admiration?*

 Affirmation

(Wife:) *I especially appreciate and admire you for . . .*

 Prayer

(Wife's prayer:)

Lord, open my eyes to see more and more the truly fine qualities of this man You have given to me. Set a guard upon my tongue, that my sometimes critical thoughts would not so often cross my lips. Remind me daily to praise and admire him....

THE FROSTING AND THE CAKE

Up to this point, we've dealt with attitudes and influences that affect the sexual relationship. We've seen how a climate of intimacy helps a woman respond sexually.

I said that for the wife, the physical union was merely the frosting on the cake. For us men, however, the act is not just the frosting—it's the cake itself! It's important for wives to accept this as normal and proper for their husbands. Strong sexual drives do not contradict spiritual maturity.

If a Christian male's sexual needs are not being fulfilled, he may experience a powerful temptation to look elsewhere. Therefore, the wife can have a tremendous ministry in her husband's life by meeting these biological needs.

With that in mind, let's focus our attention on the physical union of husband and wife.

 Bible Study

Read Genesis 2:18-25, and Genesis 1:27,28,31. Notice especially the phrases "they will become one flesh" and "it was very good." Who designed the physical union of husband and wife? What was His opinion of it? Are these passages before or after the fall?

Read Proverbs 5:15-19 (scan the whole chapter to get the context). What are the key words in vv. 18,19? What do they suggest about how God views physical love between married partners?

If the above hasn't convinced you that God intended the sexual union of husband and wife to be a pleasurable, meaningful experience —that it wasn't just something tacked on after the fall to deal with lust—turn to the Song of Solomon (also called Song of Songs). This book describes the intimate relationship between Solomon and his bride. (I highly recommend Jody Dillow's *Solomon on Sex*, a careful exposition of the Song of Solomon, coupled with practical applications for the modern marriage.) Reading aloud from the Song of Solomon is a good way to set the stage for sexual union.

"The Song of Songs celebrates the intoxicating pleasure of

Intimacy

sexual activity between two persons who are united by loving commitment," Lawrence J. Crabb, Jr., writes. "The two bodies that come together house two persons who are already together."[6]

Becoming One Flesh

Becoming "one flesh" involves the whole gamut of a relationship between man and wife. Sometimes partners who are otherwise close, however, need help in their physical relationship. They can benefit from understanding reasons for potential sexual dissatisfaction.

The following questions are designed to help you pinpoint problem areas in your sexual relationship. Before you begin, keep in mind two rules:

1. Be honest while being as gentle as possible.
2. Trust that your partner is being honest. Do not interpret what you hear as, "I am not a good lover, I have failed."

Even though you apply these rules, you still may wound each other deeply while fencing with this sensitive topic. You might want to refer to chapter 8, the section entitled "Fussin' and Forgiving," to help in maintaining forgiving attitudes.

(Note: I hope you've brought along one or two of the books recommended on the subject of sex. These questions are designed to pinpoint problems, but you will need to turn to reference works to find solutions.)

 Interaction

1. QUICK QUIZ: Each take a sheet of paper and answer the following; then share your answers.

   At the present time, the aspect I like best about our sexual relationship is . . .

   The aspect I like the least about our present sexual relationship is . . .

2. Here are some possible reasons for sexual dissatisfaction. *Which of these apply to us?*
   a. Disagreement about frequency

b. Pregnancy or new baby
c. Illness or fatigue
d. Job pressures and distractions
e. Inability to talk together about the subject
f. Personal hang-ups
g. Husband ejaculates prematurely
h. Wife doesn't experience orgasm
i. Pain in intercourse
j. Other:

Intimacy

3. Decide which one or two of the above seem to be most pressing. Skim the books you brought along. (Dr. Wheat's book contains a subject index.) Read aloud the appropriate sections and discuss how to overcome the situations that most affect your sexual relationship.

4. Each write answers separately to the following, and then discuss. As you talk, try to make specific, positive suggestions.

I feel that I would enjoy our sexual relationship more fully if you would
   a. *be more responsive*
   b. *take the initiative more often*
   c. *dress differently*
   d. *be more careful to be clean*
   e. *take more time*
   f. *pay more attention to the atmosphere created in our bedroom (candles, locked door, etc.)*
   g. *let me know that you desire me*
   h. *learn what pleases me*
   i. *be more creative in our lovemaking*
   j. *be more tender in foreplay*
   k. *not expect such a high standard of "perfect performance" from me.*
   l. *other:*

 Affirmation

I am grateful for the way in which we can enjoy one another physically. I feel especially close to you when . . .

I look forward to an increasingly deep expression of our one-flesh relationship in sexual union.

Prayer

Lord, our sexual relationship is anything but perfect. Give us freedom from the world's ideas, so that we won't demand perfection from each other. Help us to know what we should accept right now, and what we should trust You to make better. We place our physical relationship completely into Your hands. Thank You that we can talk about it openly. . .

 Action Point

Intimacy

Let's review our discussion and set one simple goal. (For example: We each will commit to making, in the area of sexual intimacy, one change requested by the other partner.) (Record your goal here and review it from time to time.)

Chapter 10

Green Thumbs Make Blueprints

The first year we tried a vegetable garden, the snails ate more salad than we did. Our neighbor informed us afterward, as she surveyed our devastated crop, that we should have planted a row of onions ringing the lettuce patch. Snails don't like the onions, she said, so our lettuce would have been protected.

Because we didn't plan, a lot of hard work yielded a very low result. Does that ever happen to you?

Many of us can identify with the pilot who announced over the intercom, "I have good news and bad news. The bad news is, we've lost all our instruments from the electrical storm and have no idea where we are. The good news is, we have a tail wind and are making excellent time!"

It's easy, isn't it, to make "excellent time" on our fast-paced trip to—-where? As Christians, we are confident of our ultimate destiny—we'll spend eternity enjoying the presence of our Lord. But does that mean we know the direction that our lives on earth should take? Not necessarily.

WHO AM I?
WHY AM I HERE?
WHERE AM I GOING?

Many non-Christians are asking these questions. Perhaps we, as Christians, should keep asking these, but on a deeper level.

"Why keep asking, if I know the answer?"

"I know where I came from, and I know where I'm going," Jesus said in John 8:14. He had a very clear sense of His life purpose. When Jesus reached the end of His life, He told His

Father that He had completed His assigned tasks (John 17:4). How did the Lord know He'd finished His life work? He had a sharp picture of what it was. And He fulfilled His purpose by living according to His *priorities*, according to the values He knew were important.

Does everyone need such a clear image of his own life purpose? No, it's not necessary at all, if our main concern is mere survival. We simply could let our lives drift from job to television to a few hours logged at the church each week. But God wants to bring honor to Himself in very specific ways through the time and talents He's given us. Aimless drifting is not a viable option for those of us in God's family.

Priorities

"It's just not me!"

"But prioritized living is just not me," some argue. "I simply don't think or operate that way."

Neither do Donna or I, all of the time. I know many Christians who say the same, yet they have learned to practice some fundamental skills of prioritizing their lives. They do not structure every single particle of their existence, but they do have an idea of where they're headed and how they want to get there. When they set goals, they know how to work them into their lives.

Take Doug, for example. He's the first to admit that living according to goals isn't his "thing." Yet after he learned some planning principles, he established and stuck to a family budget, for the first time. The budget is now a habit and continues to work smoothly.

Most of us are not goal-oriented dynamos. Even if we are, we may need to learn to prioritize not only our businesses, but also our family and personal spheres of influence.

"But if the Spirit is leading, why plan?"

Some say, "I never plan, I let the Lord lead!" Yet goal setting can facilitate the Holy Spirit's work in our lives. A goal is simply a decision, but it's a decision made *in advance* when our hearts are quiet and attentive to the Holy Spirit. It's a decision made before pressures and temptations surround us, before we get emotionally involved, before we're tired or impulsive.

Commit to the LORD whatever you do, and
your plans will succeed (Proverbs 16:4).

In his heart a man plans his course, but the LORD
determines his steps (Proverbs 16:9).

These verses show both sides of the coin. The solution isn't to throw out planning, but to be sure to commit our plans to the Lord. It's a mistake to assume that the Holy Spirit's leading is always "spontaneous," unless we revise our understanding of "spontaneity." The ice skater whose performance appears the most spontaneous is one who has practiced for many hours each day. The Christian who spontaneously leads people to Christ is usually the one who is trained and prepared to do so.

Instead of avoiding the whole process of prioritizing, goal setting and planning, we simply need to remember that the Holy Spirit is our "management consultant." We must be sure to listen to His directions at the beginning, middle and end of the planning process. That's the balance.

How do we live out priorities?

How can we begin to discover our priorities and then live according to them, yet still reflect our unique personalities? I have divided the process into three sections:
1. establishing your life priorities
2. setting goals
3. planning

First, determine where you and your mate are headed in life, which *establishes* your *life priorities*. These form a framework from which to begin. Next, considering your God-given talents, spiritual gifts, and personal hopes and desires, decide what you want to see happen within the next few months and years. Making such decisions is called *setting goals*.

It's important not only to think about your goals, but also to write them down. A study done by Harvard Business School showed a direct correlation between the income level of the persons surveyed and whether or not they had specific, written life goals. Those who had put their goals on paper reported incomes significantly higher than those who had simply thought theirs through. Of course, much more important than the financial benefits of written goals are the personal and spiritual benefits, to you and to God's kingdom!

After you've set some goals, and written them down, the third step is to examine the cause-and-effect relationship between how you're living now and how you will reach your goals. That process is called *planning*; in other words, restructuring the present to fit with what you want to see happen in the future.

Let's Begin Talking . . .

 Interaction

Priorities

QUICK QUIZ: Each match the following words and the definitions below on your own paper. The winner is the one who doesn't have to look back in the chapter to find the answers!

Words:

1._____ goal
2._____ goal-setting
3._____ planning
4._____ priorities
5._____ the Holy Spirit

Definitions:

a. Deciding what you want to accomplish over the next few months and years
b. Your "management consultant" from God
c. Values you deem important
d. Restructuring the present to fit what you want to happen in the future
e. A decision made in advance

Puffballs or God's Plans?

As you begin your own planning process, you probably will come up with some far-fetched goals, which you think you never could accomplish. You also will find yourselves writing down some that seem reasonable. Should you throw out the zany and stick to what you're pretty sure you can attain? Before you do, consider this:

Without faith it is impossible to please God (Hebrews 11:6).

Some of your wildest ideas may be sparks of new convictions

the Lord is developing in you! He may be planting in your heart the seeds of plans that you cannot possibly fulfill on your own, which He wants to fulfill through you, to His glory.

We saw this illustrated in our own lives soon after we moved to West Germany. Hordes of neighborhood kids, fascinated by our American children, frequented our home. We had no experience in and very little desire for child evangelism, but the Lord began to put in our hearts the conviction that we should reach these children with the gospel. Through a tremendously stretching series of faith steps, we held a Good News Club in our basement for two consecutive summers. At the conclusion, nine German children said they'd like to know Jesus personally. The goal and its results far exceeded our own capabilities.

In his helpful book, *Faith Planning*, Bruce Cook warns of the pitfalls of "projection planning." This means assessing what's happened in the past and relying on present resources to pull it off again. He also counsels against "wishful planning," in which a Christian simply responds emotionally to some exciting challenge.[1] Find a balance between these two extremes. Don't throw out your wild ideas, but let the Lord show you over a period of time if they are mere emotional puff balls, or the first seeds of His plans.

Here's an overview of the two sections that follow:

PHASE I: Clarifying your priorities and setting goals.

  A: SET YOUR SAIL: You'll examine Paul's life priorities and formulate your own.
  B: SHARPENING DREAMS INTO GOALS: You'll indulge in some creative dreaming. Then you'll pare down these dreams into some long-range goals that complement your life priorities.

PHASE II: Shaping goals into reality.

  MOVING FROM HERE TO THERE: You'll look on as one couple goes through a five-step process of ordering their lives in accordance with the goals they have set. Then it's your turn to do the same!

Please don't succumb to the temptation to skip over the Bible study sections. The process is as important as the final outcome. You'll be walking through a procedure that can become woven into your lifestyle.

PHASE I:
A. SET YOUR SAIL

Priorities

Definition: A *life priority* is something that has the right to take precedence over the other elements in one's life. It is not necessarily discovered by asking, "Upon what do I spend the most time?" but rather, "Upon what do I want to concentrate the creative energies of my life?"

 Interaction

But seek first His kingdom and His righteousness, and all these things will be given to you as well (Matthew 6:33).

Take some time to think in broad terms about your priorities, the things with the "right to take precedence" over the elements of your life. Use the above Scripture as a framework for your thinking.

Take two pages from your Talkbook and tear each into six equal parts, so that you have 12 slips of paper. Write on each one the name of a life category. Some examples:

GOD (i.e., my relationship with Him)
SPOUSE   WORK   SELF
CHILDREN   RELATIVES
MATERIAL EXTRAS   the WORLD (non-Christians in my
the BODY (other believers)   sphere of influence)

Then each, in turn, take the slips of paper and put them in a certain configuration, according to the order of priority you feel they have in your life. You may come up with a list, a chart or a group of circles; you may see these priorities as immutable or in a constant state of flux. Explain to your partner why you have arranged the slips as you have.

 Bible Study

In 2 Corinthians 5:14-20, Paul outlines the ways his life

priorities changed after becoming a Christian. Read the passage aloud. List Paul's life priorities as seen in these verses (see also Philippians 3:7-10). Write your observations in your Talkbook.

The following verses apply to all Christians and imply God's choices of priorities for our lives. Look up the verses and list in your Talkbook the "life priorities" suggested by each: Colossians 1:9,10; Galatians 5:13,14, 23; Matthew 28:19,20; Philippians 2:4-8.

Example: Colossians 1:9,10:
1. Live a life worthy of the Lord.
2. Grow in the knowledge of God.

 Interaction

(Optional exercise: "WHO AM I?" A certain amount of self-knowledge is necessary before attempting to formulate priorities and goals. If you feel the need, take a few moments to brainstorm together about your individual talents, abilities, likes and dislikes, strengths and weaknesses. Record in your Talkbook.)

You now have in your Talkbook a list of life priorities that all Christians hold in common—whether or not they are aware of it. In addition, you will want to think of priorities that are uniquely your own, such as:
1. *Developing and using my God-given talents and interests in the areas of:*
2. *Being used by the Lord to minister to the following specific target groups:*
3. *Being a husband/wife who, by my attitudes and actions, fosters the development of my mate.*
4. *Raising and discipling my children into mature Christians who can lead others to Christ.*

Each take a sheet from your Talkbook and spend five minutes writing down some phrases that express your individual life priorities. Just get your first ideas down; you can revise later. Keep them broad and general, yet be more specific than "to glorify God." List several that are common to all Christians and several that are unique to you.

Now compare and discuss what you have written. Take a few minutes to help each other revise and rewrite, until each of you is satisfied that the result reflects the person God is causing you to become.

If your life priority lists seem incompatible, you definitely have grounds for prayer! You each are two different individuals, with unique contributions to make to the body of Christ, yet the Lord wants your hearts to be united in a desire to live for Him.

> ...make my joy complete by being like-minded, having the same love, being one in spirit and purpose (Philipians 2:2)

Priorities

 Affirmation

I am encouraged as I see a glimpse of what God might want us to become. I want to stand with you so that, together, we may be all that He has designed us to be.

 Prayer

Father, the life priorities we have written sound so overwhelming to us. We are two very inadequate creatures with some ideas, but little power to see them become reality. Help us live each day in the power of Your Holy Spirit, that we might think Your thoughts and that Your dreams for us might come true. Guide us now as we continue to think and dream. . .

PHASE I:
B. SHARPENING DREAMS INTO GOALS

You have decided on some overall general priorities for each of your lives. The next step is to set some detailed long-range goals. But before you do, I'd like you to indulge in a creative exercise.

Each take a blank sheet from your Talkbook and label it "My Wildest Dreams." Working independently, write down your secret desires and ambitions—the things you would most like to do and be, assuming you had limitless spiritual, financial, personal and time resources. Put absolutely no limits on yourself here; let your imagination run free. Think in the context of your family as a unit as well as yourself as an individual. The only criterion is that you write down what you personally desire.

 ## Interaction

Compare your lists. Are there some surprises? Perhaps you see your spouse in a new light after learning his or her secret ambitions!

Now spend some time comparing your "wildest dreams" with the life priorities you just formulated. Do you see gaps and inconsistencies? Discuss together.

It's important to dream big, but equally important to lay our dreams on God's altar. God Himself has a big dream—to bring a lost world back to Himself (Luke 19:10). When we lay our own ambitions at the foot of the cross, we begin to see the world through Jesus' eyes. God may begin reshaping our dreams to make His dream for us come true.[2]

Donna experienced this in her long-standing dream of being used of God as a writer. Several years ago she began planning to study for an advanced degree at a British university. At the same time, she spent extended periods with the Lord to lay her dreams into His hands.

Over the span of several months, God increasingly burdened her with the spiritual needs in Europe, where she was then living. She returned to the United States and joined the staff of Campus Crusade; not long afterward, we married and moved to Europe.

For a long time it looked as though her original dream of being a writer had been shelved. Now the Lord is beginning to make that dream come true, but the details surrounding it are very different from what she had imagined.

 ## Prayer

Take a few moments together, to put your dreams before the Lord. Admit your desires. Ask Him to weigh, sift and refine, so that your desires become the ones He would most like you to have. Ask Him to lead you now, as you set specific goals. Pray:

Lord Jesus, if You were me, what would you be planning in the power of the Holy Spirit?

All a man's ways seem innocent to him, but motives are weighed by the LORD (Proverbs 16:2).

Priorities

Discovering your dreams is important. It's also vital to sift through your dreams, and temporarily shelve the ones that don't move you toward where you want to go. Those that remain can be viewed as goals, to be pursued with prayer and determination.

It's not really a matter of "where do I want to go?" but rather "where does He want to take me?"[3]

 Bible Study

Priorities

Read aloud 1 Corinthians 9:24-26. If achieving your lifetime priorities will earn you a "prize," what implications does this have for setting life goals? Write your ideas in your Talkbook.

Now let's set some specific life goals in several areas. Each take a few blank sheets. You will fill out a Personal Goals Survey, according to the following pattern:

PERSONAL GOALS SURVEY[4]

I. Priorities: *My life priorities are:*

II. Goals: *Ten years from today, if the above are truly priorities in my life, I could observe the following about myself:*

A. *I would have achieved (specific accomplishments):*

B. *These personal and spiritual characteristics would have been developed in my life (qualities such as greater patience, good physical condition, being devoted to prayer, etc.):*

C. *I would be involved in the following type of work and have these responsibilities:*

D. *My income would be $ _____ /year (disregarding the influence of probable inflation).*

E. *The following characteristics would describe my relationship with my spouse:*

F. *I would observe the following characteristics in my family:*

G. *My involvement in my community/church would take the form of:*

H. *I might be pursuing the following hobbies or interests for personal enrichment:*

 **Interaction**

Copy your revised life priority statements under number I.

Now look at your dream sheets. Which of those dreams might you attain during the next ten years, keeping in mind that nothing is too hard for God (Jeremiah 32:17)? Working consecutively, write them under the appropriate headings on your Personal Goals Surveys. Leave several lines blank at the end of each section for additions.

Do not include dreams that do not seem to contribute toward fulfilling your overall life priority. For example, a desire to buy a sailboat and spend a year sailing doesn't seem consistent with an overall priority of wanting to be an ambassador for Christ in the business world. Keep it on your dream sheet and re-evaluate it next year!

Also omit any dreams that you're pretty sure are mere fantasies. (I've always dreamed about being an opera singer, but if you've ever heard me sing, you know in what category that belongs!) Don't be afraid to pursue a hobby or special interest, however, even if it isn't "spiritual." These can enrich our lives and add greatly to our overall well-being and that of those around us.

Take several more minutes to add to the eight categories under number II any other ideas which come to mind. Ask:

If the statements under number I really are my priorities, what difference will that make in each of these areas?

Then, share with each other what you have written. Discuss and refine. You may want to borrow from each other's lists. Don't worry if you aren't totally satisfied with the results.

Priorities

You now have formulated and written down some long-range goals for your life. According to the Harvard Survey, that puts you in the upper 3 percent of the population! But remember, "Goals … shouldn't be viewed as end products. Goals are useful only as they help us move from here toward somewhere else."[5]

 Prayer

Father, again we feel very small as we see where we want our lives to be headed. Apart from Your help, these desires will be just nice-sounding words. Remind us every day to draw on Your power to complete the task You have given us . . .

PHASE II:
MOVING FROM HERE TO THERE

You may have been muttering under your breath, "It's fine and dandy to set all these lofty goals, but what use is it? The Vanns ought to live in our home for a week—they'd see how fast our nice goals can fly out the window! It's probably easy for them; they are surely very disciplined people. But for me and my mate, following through on goals is impossible!"

If you have been thinking something like that, you've hit upon an essential point: *A goal never translated into action is worse than no goal at all.* It's worse, because failure to live up to one's own expectations plasters a layer of guilt over the frustration of aimless living.

You'd be wrong, by the way, to assume that we Vanns are disciplined. Although we have a lot of *persistence,* which is a great help in achieving goals, we don't have a lot of *self-discipline.* The only way we've seen some of our long-term goals become present realities is *through reducing long-range goals to short-range measureable parts and scheduling them into our calendars.*

This is the process called *planning*. Time-management experts define planning as "bringing the future into the present."[6]

When Donna is at home all day with our two youngest children (ages two and four), she quickly develops a crisis/reaction mentality. She runs from the telephone to the skinned knee to the spilled milk to the soup boiling over to the training-pants failure. That is fairly normal for a mother of preschoolers. And, realistically, all of the above activities ultimately contribute toward Donna's goal of wanting to raise godly children. But when Christians run their whole lives in crisis/reaction patterns, the results are ineffective, unfruitful, and often chaotic lives.

Order Your Life According to the Goal

First, take a "goal check": Do you genuinely feel strongly about your goals, or are they faked imitations of someone else's goals? If you are lukewarm about certain goals, yet believe they are from the Lord, ask Him to turn up the flame!

Look at what you have written on your Personal Goals Survey. Put stars beside the goals that you feel the most deeply about. You'll want to concentrate your first efforts on these.

 Bible Study

Read aloud Hebrews 12:1-3 and Philippians 3:12-17. In what ways do the writers recommend that Christians follow through on their goals? (Discuss and write key phrases in your Talkbook.)

How will you apply the insights from the above verses? This proven five-step process can help you translate your long-range goals into reality:

1. Reduce long-term goals to measurable short-term goals.

2. Reduce each short-term goal to one or more specific activities.

3. Block the specific activities into your calendar.

4. Look at your calendar daily and do what it says!

5. Modify, pray and press on.

Step One: Reduce long-term goals to measurable short-term goals.

Some examples:

A. FINANCIAL
  Long-term goal: Earn more money.
  Short-term goal: Earn $5,000 more next year.

B. SPIRITUAL
  Long-term goal: Have God's Word become more a part of my life.
  Short-term goal: Read the whole Bible in one year.
  Short-term goal: Memorize one Bible verse per week.

C. FAMILY
  Long-term goal: Have a closer relationship with my wife.
  Short-term goal: During the next six months spend more time together than we presently do.
  Short-term goal: Over the next six months, learn to show love to my wife in ways that are meaningful to her.

Remember, short-term goals need to be specific, limited in time and measureable. At the end of the time limit you've set, you should be able to look back and clearly see if you reached your short-term goal.

Step Two: Reduce each short-term goal to one or more specific activities.

The following are a few specific activities that might be listed for the three examples in Step One:

A. FINANCIAL
  - Take a training course that will give me expertise in an additional area of in my profession.
  - Weed out my non-paying clientele and concentrate on productive customers.

B. SPIRITUAL
  - Each day before breakfast, spend fifteen minutes reading the Bible, following a daily reading chart.

C. FAMILY
  - Take my wife out (minus kids) two evenings a month
  - During the next six months, go away together for one marriage retreat weekend.

Step Three: Block the specific activities onto your calendar.

Donna and I each have a calendar that we use in planning and we keep them handy at all times. I prefer one that gives a whole month, with a square for each day. Donna likes one week per page, with space on each day for her daily "to do" list. We also record activities involving both of us on a monthly calendar, which we keep by the telephone.

For me, a short-term goal is about as permanent as cotton candy until I translate it into an activity on my calendar. Once there, it is etched in concrete (although I do write in pencil!), unless I have a very good reason to change it.

Step Four: Look at your calendar daily and do what it says!

This step is obvious, but it is where many of us fall down. For starters, put your open calendar in some spot where you'd have to close your eyes not to see it.

To break the calendar-avoidance syndrome, try not to over-plan. You'll only become discouraged. Psychologically it may be better to have a two-item "to-do" list, which you totally complete, than a ten-item list, of which you accomplish four.

And don't write down all your daily drudgeries on your calendar—the things you'll do automatically anyway. That's demotivating! Only write down a drudgery such as fifteen minutes of daily exercise, when you are first attempting to work it into your life. After it's stuck, don't force yourself to keep seeing it on your calendar.

Step Five: Pray, modify and press on.

Life changes; plans must change also. It is discouraging, though, when you've spent time planning, but everything falls through. That's when it's good to remember Who is really in charge of your plans!

Even if everything changes, it's still essential to plan. As the adage goes, "If you don't plan your life, somebody else will!" When you have in mind where you want to go, you can still get there, even if you have to take a different route than you originally thought. You'll be more aware of your options and can adapt to change.

Priorities

Donna and I try to set aside each Sunday evening before bed as planning time. We plan separately, then compare notes. After all, if she's counting on an evening out with me, I'd better have it on my calendar. If I'm inviting some friends over to watch football, it shouldn't be on the night she wants to have a Family Fun Time.

Priorities

Donna and I also have agreed to be accountable to each other in areas of personal development. Has she been keeping up with her aerobics? Have I been having my daily quiet time with the Lord? We consider ways to help each other act upon our good intentions. (For this to be productive, you need to maintain a healthy grace-relationship with yourself, your spouse and the Lord. Review chapter 3 if necessary.)

Because of the unexpected, it takes real persistence to achieve goals. That's why Paul's advice in Philippians 3:12-14 is so pertinent: Forget the past and press on. And only the Lord can give that kind of persistence!

Let's Take a Practice Run

In this chapter you have been given a method to translate long-term goals into reality. Perhaps you shouldn't try to do that now with every area on your Personal Goals Survey. You'd feel swamped and probably never find a calendar with enough days! So let's pick one area and work through it.

As an example, let's take a couple we know, whom we'll call Rick and Diane. Because the area of "job" is not dealt with elsewhere in this book, and because it is a mammoth topic that profoundly shapes our whole lives, we'll look on as Rick does some specific planning related to items C and D, under section II - Goals, on his Personal Goals Survey. Rick currently is working two construction jobs and, in his free time, ministers to youth at his church. The church has an opening for a full-time youth pastor, however, for which Rick may apply.

The first part of Rick's Personal Goals Survey might look like this:

I. Priorities: My life priorities are:
- *to live a holy life, that others might see Christ in me;*
- *to be a Christ-honoring husband and father;*
- *to help young people meet Christ, grow in their faith and become spiritual multipliers.*

II. Goals: Ten years from today, if the above were truly priorities in my life, I could observe the following about myself: (Remember we are looking at C and D so are skipping A and B.)

C. I would be involved in the following type of work and have these responsibilities:
- *more extensive evangelism and discipleship with youth;*
- *a job that provides adequate income to meet our financial needs, especially in light of wanting another child.*

D. My income would be $_____/year. *Not important, as long as physical needs are being met.*

Here is how Rick and his wife might apply the five-step planning process to reach his stated goal of wanting to work more with youth:

Step One: Reduce long-term goals to short-term measurable goals.

Should Rick change his job to fit his long-term goal of winning youth? Diane might have hesitations, such as their future financial security. What will be his salary? Is there a pension plan?

One approach they could use to clarify their thinking is a pro-con sheet. Through this method, the Lord can direct decision-making and give the "sound judgment" He promises in 2 Timothy 1:7. Their sheet might look like this:

Full-Time Youth Pastor

PRO	CON
• Meets my lifetime objective, which my present job does not • I would enjoy doing it • I feel it's something I have a "gift" for • Would enrich our family, since it's something we could all share in together • Relieves stress of giving the Lord my "tired hours"	• Might mean less financial security and therefore insecurity for Diane • Could be very demanding on time and emotions • Question: Could we ever buy a house?

If Rick can favorably answer the question about the house, and Diane gives a green light, he and Diane probably will continue to pursue this job change. If God is leading Rick to such a ministry, He will confirm it through any or all of the following: (1) peace within, (2) godly counsel, (3) confirming circumstances and (4) sound reasoning.

Priorities

Note that Rick's present job is not very challenging, nor is he motivated by the thought of making a lot of money. If he does not go into full-time Christian work, he will want to continue re-evaluating his present job in light of what they want to see God do with their lives. Perhaps he should seek changes within his current jobs or look for another secular job. Or maybe he will continue with the same jobs, but with his priorities and goals firmly in mind.

If Rick does decide to pursue the position at church, he reduces his long-term goal of "working with youth" to the short-term goal, "Pursue youth pastor job." He now breaks this down into the following activities:

Step Two: Reduce each short-term goal to one or more specific activities.

1. Meet with _____ (an impartial, mature believer) to discuss this.
2. Call to schedule a meeting with church committee to discuss ministry philosophy. (At that meeting, ask about provision of house.)
3. Prepare youth evangelism and discipleship plan, which I can present at same meeting.
4. Spend half of next Saturday alone with the Lord, thinking and praying about changing jobs.

Step Three: Block the specific activities onto your calendar.

Rick notes on his next day's "to-do" list to call his friend and the church committee chairman. Since he knows the committee meets one month from now, he marks off one evening each week for the next three weeks to work on his youth evangelism and discipleship plan, which he will present at that meeting. After he's checked his calendar against Diane's, he also writes in the half-day of prayer on Saturday.

Steps Four and Five: Carry them through!

Remember The Five Steps

You can use these practical steps again and again to whittle dreams into realities.

1. Reduce long-term goals to measurable short-term goals.
2. Reduce each short-term goal to one or more specific activities.
3. Block the specific activities onto your calendar.
4. Look at your calendar daily and do what it says!
5. Modify, pray and press on.

One last word: Talking about goals and priorities may give some the feeling that we're striving for some sort of super-life, free from the commonplace of "just" living. But life consists of eating, sleeping, changing diapers, running errands, reading a good book. . . none of which are unspiritual if done in a Christ-honoring way. We want to examine the way we live, however, and keep our goals in view, so that we do not simply wander aimlessly, but instead see God's purposes for us being accomplished.

 Interaction

Talk about which one of your long-term goals you could begin to translate into reality. For now, pick one that you can work on together. Write down your ideas, steps and action plans in your Talkbook and then on your calendars. After you've gotten into the swing of some new habit patterns, say in about six months, tackle another goal in a similar way on your next marriage retreat.

 Affirmation

I appreciate the way the Holy Spirit is working in your life. I don't want to get in His way, yet I want to encourage you to pursue your goals. I need your encouragement also, because sometimes I forget, or I lose motivation. Let's talk about some ways we can constructively remind each other to press on toward the goals we have set. (Record your ideas.)

Prayer

Lord, we are glad that You are such a great God. Thank You for the abilities You've given us, and for the gift of time. Give us the wisdom to make right choices as we continue to plan our lives, and the power of Your Spirit to make Your best plans for us come true. . .

Priorities **Action Point**

Let's review our discussion and set one simple goal. (If you applied the Five Steps to one of your long-range goals, you have completed your action point for this chapter.)

Chapter 11
"You Spent OUR Money on a Weed-Zapper?"

Finances

"Sure, I bought a weed-zapper," the husband admits. "But we really needed it! My time is too valuable to do all that trimming by hand."

"But, Honey!" his wife wails. "I can think of ten things that are more essential. An exercise bike, for example. Why didn't you discuss it with me first?"

Whether rich or poor, probably every couple has had disagreements about where their income should go. These differences are so complex, with so many contingent side issues, that money problems are counted as a major cause in half of all divorces today.[1]

The important thing isn't so much that a "Tanya Tightwad" and a "Spencer Spend-it-all" have a moderating influence on each other, although that may happen for the good of their marriage. Most of all, Tanya and Spencer need to develop the mind of Christ about the issue of money and material posessions.

How do we gain the mind of Christ about a particular concern? By first making sure that we are walking with the Holy Spirit, and then asking the Spirit to give us wisdom as we search God's Word. (See 1 Corinthians 2:10-16.)

God obviously wants to communicate with us on the subject of money—it is mentioned about seven hundred times in the Bible. Nearly two-thirds of Christ's parables concern the use of money. "God equates our use of wealth with our commitment to Him."[2]

Because of the abundance of financial planning material currently available for Christians, this chapter is brief. As you discuss the questions included here, you should be able to pinpoint some of your differences, and then zero in on God's perspective of possessions. For specifies on budgeting, climbing out of debt and so on, use one of the excellent books recommended in the bibliography. Chapter 10 in this book offers general guidelines on prioritizing, goal-setting and seeing goals become part of your daily lives. The issues raised in that chapter provide a helpful context for this whole area of finances.

Let's Begin Talking...

Finances

 Interaction

(Each take a blank sheet of paper and complete the following:)

1. *The thing that bothers me the most about my spouse's attitude toward money and possessions is . . .*

2. *A recent purchase I did not agree to was . . .*

3. *An item I wish we had purchased was . . .*

   Compare and discuss your answers. Now consider some possible root causes of financial difficulties. Discuss which may apply to each of you.

Root causes of financial problems:
1. Self-indulgence—attempting to make up for emotional lacks in other areas.
2. Insecurity—attempting to protect against the uncertainty of the future through impulse buying or excessive thrift.
3. Ostentation—desire to impress others by having just as much or more.
4. Feelings of superiority—an attitude of "I deserve the best."
5. Low self-esteem—surrounding yourselves with things in order to hide an inferiority complex.
6. Greed—love of money which overshadows your love for God.

Where Do Couples Get Off The Track?

 Bible Study

   Look up the following verses and read aloud. In the Talkbook make a list of the wrong attitudes toward money and possessions as seen in these verses: Matthew 6:31,32; Luke 16:13; 1 John

2:15-17; Deuteronomy 1 8:10-14; 1 Timothy 6:9,10.
Do any of these passages speak to our situation?

 Interaction

Financial planning experts say that couples tend to experience financial difficulties in the following areas:

1. Lack of communication (for example: husband makes out budget but does not ask wife's input).
2. Confusion over who should be in charge of what. (One writer claims that in 90 percent of all homes, the wife keeps the books![3])
3. Getting into "financial bondage" (i.e., monthly payments exceeding monthly income).
4. Not having a workable budget, or not following it if one exists.
5. Bad financial decisions (an unwise investment, for example, or buying a home too quickly).

Do you see yourselves on this list? Would you add other problem areas? In the Talkbook make a list of "Financial Difficulties" that you want to resolve, the dates you propose to discuss these, and the books you will use as resources.

 Affirmation

I feel I can learn from you in the area of dealing with possessions when I observe you . . .

 Prayer

Lord, help us to accept, understand and appreciate each other, even though we may approach money differently. As we continue to seek Your perspective on material posessions, we both want to be sure that we are filled with your Holy Spirit...

The First Step Toward Financial Freedom

"Couples who wish to get their finances squared away must—I repeat, must—seek the counsel of Scripture."

(Charles Swindoll)[4]

Bible Study

Read aloud Job 1:21. What does it suggest about the ultimate ownership of your money and possessions? Read Job 42:12. Does God view your possessions as "unspiritual"? When do possessions become a problem? (see Matthew 6:24)

If God retains ownership of our money and posessions, then we are simply stewards. A "steward" can be defined as a manager, or as someone who has been given a trust. (Jesus' parable of the ten talents in Luke 19:11-26 expands on this concept.)

Finances

God's intention is for His stewards to seek Him first, to give generously, and to trust Him to meet their material needs.

Read aloud four passages which illustrate the above: Matthew 6:33, 1 Timothy 6:6-8; 2 Corinthians 9:6-8; Philippians 4:16,17,19.

Putting God first, giving generously as he directs and trusting Him for daily essentials allows financial peace to reign. That peace is the first step toward financial freedom.

 Interaction

What does the statement, "God will meet our needs," mean to us?

In the Talkbook make three columns, "Needs," "Wants," and "Undecided." Discuss together the possessions that you want to acquire, and attempt to place them in one of the three categories. For example:

NEEDS	WANTS	UNDECIDED
adequate living quarters	home ownership	new stylish clothes

(God often supplies many of our *wants*; but at times He may meet only our basic *needs*.)

Let's discuss:
How hard are we willing to work for the items in the "wants" column?

How do we weigh the financial gain from extra work against possible loss of family togetherness?

When we apply the test question, "What would bring the

most honor to the Lord in this situation?" what insights do we gain?

Do we want to make any changes in the type or amount of work either of us is doing?

 ## Affirmation

Even though we have had financial misunderstandings in the past, I am trusting that the Holy Spirit now is working in each of us to produce a spirit of unity.

 ## Prayer

A Prayer Covenant

Lord, we covenant together now in Your presence to seek You first, to put You ahead of any material gain. We accept the fact that we are simply temporary managers of the money and possessions You have given us. We want to give generously to others under Your leadership. We trust You to meet our daily needs and to lead us into financial freedom . . .

Signed: _____

Signed: _____

Date: _____

 ## Action Point

Let's review our discussion and set one simple goal. (For example: Using a financial planning book recommended in the bibliography to help us, we will spend one evening a week for the next month setting up a family budget.)

Chapter 12

Nurturing Your Young Olive Plants

Child Raising

As a friend of ours remarked ruefully, "The only problem with my children is that they persist in acting like kids!"

If only we could pack our offspring into neat, smudge-free, sinless, predictable little boxes—life might become dull, but just think how much easier child raising would be!

Instead, it is a challenge from day one on. You buy your darling baby a fancy backpack, but he refuses to ride on anyone's back. That's your first clue: the kid isn't going to go by the books.

Somewhere along mid-infancy it hits you (probably about 3 a.m., when you're holding a squalling baby over one arm and frantically thumbing through Dr. Spock's manual with your free hand). The whole mess is out of your control! As a parent, you have hit rock-bottom in the well of adequacy, and you begin to wallow around down there in the goo of guilt.

Because of this experience, so common to parenthood, this chapter begins by confronting the emotional needs of parents. The chapter is divided into three parts:

Section   I - You and I, the Parents (how we feel and what we can do about it)

Section   II - They, the Children (their needs for discipline, training and love)

Section III - We, the Family (visualizing and working toward the future; planning family times)

Let's Begin Talking . . .

YOU AND I, THE PARENTS

 **Interaction**

Each take a sheet from your Talkbook. In a few sentences, complete the following:

For me, the most difficult thing about being a parent is . . .

Child Raising

The part of parenthood that brings me the most joy and fulfillment is . . .

Share your answers with each other.

Being a parent is an overwhelming task. It's made even more so by the "guilt goons"—those charter members of the emotional Mafia who slink around in your home making sure that you pay and pay and pay . . .

"You mean to say you don't memorize Scripture with your children?" They whisper in shocked voices. "When was the last time you had a family night? . . . Isn't that boy ever going to be potty trained? . . . That daughter of yours just wiped her nose on her arm again! . . . What a terrible parent you are!"

This is not to say that we throw out Scripture memory, family nights or child training, but that we do throw out the guilt goons. It's one thing for the Holy Spirit to tap us on the shoulder and remind us of something, but the goons simply nag us! And they always end on the same note: "What a failure you are as a parent!"

The cycle goes something like this:

A fatigued mother is having a bad day, and she explodes in irritation at her children. Instead of immediately claiming the Lord's forgiveness and saying, "Kids, I'm sorry. Mommy is very tired today," she mutters inwardly, "I'm a terrible parent because I yell at my children."

The goons need no further cue. "You're absolutely right!" they chime in. "In fact, you're worse than Mrs. X down the street, and she isn't even a Christian!"

At this, the mother is overcome by intense feelings of guilt, with the probable result that she will be even more irritable with her children that day.

Sometimes the goons multiply after you've read a good Christian book on child raising. Sad to say, a few of the best authors, including some in our bibliography, come close to implying that they are succeeding most of the time as parents, and that their children are models of perfection. For those of us who experience seventeen major parenting failures before lunchtime, their examples can be bitter pills to swallow.

Accept the Valleys With the Mountains

It can be very helpful, however, to observe other children of similar ages to your own. You'll find things to marvel at, as well as things that will drive you bananas, because that's how kids are!

For example, at our home during one week:
— Lisa was sassy.
— David had several potty accidents (at age 3-1/2).
— Millay threw herself on the floor in tantrums several times.

Yet, during the same week:
— Without any outside motivation, Lisa taught herself to play the guitar.
— David asked what it meant to have Jesus in his heart.
— Millay was sunny and cheerful (between tantrums).

Children's behavior often follows a roller-coaster pattern, but don't let it put you on one!

 Interaction

In your Talkbook make two columns: "mountains" and "valleys." *Let's talk about some of the ups and downs that our children have been demonstrating lately. How have we responded to these?* (Record your observations.)

What Color Is Redemption?

Aside from accepting the ups and downs, perhaps the best way to conquer the guilt goons is to see the family as "the practice field of the Lord's redeeming grace."

Redemption means being saved, rescued or delivered from

whatever might hold us back from being all God wants us to be. But what does redemption in the Christian family look like? As a friend remarked, "Redemption in the family looks very different from what we expect." Some Christians visualize it as a beautiful, white plush carpet: a picture of spotless perfection. Personally, I've never met a family like that, and if one exists, I imagine it would be very static and sterile.

Child Raising

I think that, rather than being white, redemption in the family is the color of our dining room rug—a not-too-appetizing combination of shades resembling smashed peas, applesauce, crackers and cherry jelly. No matter what our kids drop during meals, the stains just blend right in. I believe that the outworking of the Lord's deliverance in the Christian family is like that rug—a little ugly in places, but tough, workable, real.

Edith Schaeffer, in a recent magazine interview, commented: "A mother should explain to her children, 'I'm not perfect, your dad isn't perfect, none of us is perfect. We're a lot of imperfect people living under one roof for just a limited number of years. But the reward of continuity in family life is worth working for.'"[1]

How do you catch hold of the Lord's redeeming grace in your family? Where's the receiver that will pipe it into your living room? Redemption becomes a reality through prayer; consistent, concentrated prayer for each child. The more you pray, the more you are set free from fear and guilt to be parents who operate with the help of God.

After all, we are merely His tools in the child-raising process. He will use not only us, but many other people as well to mold our children into mature adults. This is one reason it is so important to be in close contact with others in the body of Christ—they have so much to offer our children!

 Bible Study

Read aloud Philippians 4:4-7. *Let's talk about how we can regularly bring our natural anxieties about our children before the Lord, that we might experience the "peace of God" regarding them.*

"Prayer is the work of God. It is the single most important thing you can do in discipling your children. Begin in prayer, continue in prayer, and end in prayer."[2]

 **Interaction**

Perhaps the Lord's redeeming grace has been present in our family in ways we have not noticed. Thinking over the past few months, what evidences of redemption do we see? (For example: a parent reacted in anger, but then asked the child's forgiveness; a negative trait you've prayed about for months seems to be lifting, or you have more grace to accept it, and so on.)

Now let's interact about those close to us in the body of Christ. What specific things do they have to offer our children? Do we have something we can give (teaching a skill, for example) to their children?

 Affirmation

Say aloud to each other:
    I am not a perfect parent.
    I never will be perfect.
    Our children never will be perfect.
    I trust God to bring His redemption to our family in the midst
        of our imperfections.

 Prayer

Father, we as parents need to live each day, each minute, yielded to You. Teach us to walk moment-by-moment in the power of Your Spirit, that our lives and our family might bring honor to You. Remind us to pray daily for our children . . .

THEY, THE CHILDREN

"The Diamond"
A diamond in the rough
Is a diamond sure enough
For before it ever sparkles
It is made of diamond stuff.

Of course someone must find it
Or it never will be found
And someone must grind it
Or it never will be ground.

But when it's found, and when it's ground,
And when it's burnished bright
That diamond's everlasting,
Just flashing out its light.

—Author unknown

Child Raising

Our little diamonds do need cutting and polishing to outgrow their natural roughness. Yet our ultimate goal is not just that our children would become well-rounded, mature adults, but that they also would shine brightly for Christ.

We know that our children will one day take their places on the spiritual battlefield. Will they be able to "stand firm" (Ephesians 6:14)? Will they be disciples of the Lord Jesus, able to lead and teach others? (See the bibliography for books on developing Christian character in children.)

How do we help our children become all that God intends? Our primary "tool" is love.

Love is Something You Do

So runs the title of a book by our pastor in Houston. A gold mine of truth is in those words, especially when applied to children (although telling them you love them is great, too!).

Often the best defense against our natural tendencies to nag, scold and discourage our children, is a good offense: developing positive habits of loving and building them up. Discuss various expressions of love, and record in your Talkbook some specific, practical ways to make these become real in your day-to-day family life. Each evening at bedtime, you may need a "love-check" on the order of "Have you hugged your kid today?" Help each other turn your good ideas into life habits.

Out of all the many things parents can do to show love for their children, let's focus on four:
Discipline
Touching base
Building memories
Family councils

Discipline

The subject usually labeled "discipline" has two parts: discipline and training. "Discipline is primarily intended to instill obedience. Training is designed to teach social behavior, skills, and responsibility."[3]

Different methods apply to each. Spanking, for example, should be confined primarily to the area of discipline and not used as a method of training.

Bible Study

Read aloud Proverbs 13:24; 22:15; 23:13,14; 29:15,17. *What conclusions can we draw about spanking as one means of child discipline?* (Note: the term "rod" probably referred to a flexible wooden switch.)

Dr. Dobson writes, "Nature has provided a wonderfully padded place for use in moments of haughty defiance, and I wish the disciplinary 'experts' were less confused as to its proper purpose."[4]

Interaction

Read aloud from the sections on child discipline and training from one of the recommended books. Underline or copy in your Talkbook passages that seem most helpful. Discuss the following and record in your Talkbook (making it specific to each child):

1. *What new insights have we gained in discipline and training?*
2. *In what specific ways could we begin to implement these in our home? In other words, for each child, we are saying, "The next time _____ happens, we will _____,"* or, *"We will help him/her learn _____ by doing _____.* (Be sure to define the limits exactly and determine to band together in enforcing them.

Bible Study

Read aloud Ephesians 6:4, preferably in two different versions. Discuss what this means in regard to your particular family. *In what ways may we have been "exasperating" our children?*

Touching Base

Touching base with your children simply means keeping your eyes, and ears and heart open, on their level. Look at them, listen to them, draw them out, spend time talking to them; there's hardly any stronger way to say "I love you."

It also involves getting into their worlds. When our two youngest first visited "Oma" (Grandma Reid) in Texas, they immediately located her bathroom. With heads bent together, they gazed wide-eyed into the toilet bowl and shouted, "There's water in there!" (Yes, folks, German toilets are different!) They were thrilled to share with us their discovery. And every so often during our visit one of them would disappear and there'd be a telltale *KA-WOOSH* from the back of the house. What excitement!

Child Raising

I hope your kids are into something a little more high-class than toilets, but whatever it is, get right down on your knees and enjoy it with them.

 Interaction

Are we spending enough time talking and really listening to our children? Do we know what they think about, what their inner struggles are? Do we need to linger with them at bedtime? (In a darkened room kids often say things that they would not reveal elsewhere!)

What is the best time for us to touch base with them each day? Do we need to re-evaluate any job or schedules in the light of our childrens' needs?

Building Memories

Building memories needs little explanation, and I'm sure you already do it. Kids revel in special traditions and little things that always happen a certain way.

For example, after our prayer at every meal, we continue to hold hands and we lift them up and down while we repeat in German, "Let's have a happy mealtime; enjoy your food." We might as well try to eat standing on our heads as to omit that ritual even once!

 Interaction

Are there memories we could be building? Traditions that we could weave into our family fabric? Are we taking enough

pictures and slides and showing them to the kids? Do we need to add to the typical things we always do at important seasons? What about the memories of unexpected "serendipity" outings?

Family Councils

Family councils are special meetings of either the whole family or the parents and one particular child. Not to be confused with a "family fun night", a family council is more serious in nature, usually involving one or two items of business.

Anyone—parent or child—may call a family council at any time. We've had councils on such diverse subjects as Improving a Certain Young Lady's Attitude Toward Homework (called by us) and When Can I have a Guinea Pig? (called by Lisa). We keep a little notebook in which we record the decisions of the council.

The beauty of the family council is that it totally removes the need for nagging and angry outbursts. The children enter into the decision-making process; they can be reminded, if need be, of the decision that was reached. (We still retain 51 percent of the vote. As our thirteen-year-old moves into full teenagerhood, I imagine that at times we'll continue to retain the right of veto, and at other times we'll let the decision rest with her.)

Another value of the council is that children are learning, under the guidance of their parents, how decisions are made.

 Interaction

Do we need to begin having family councils? What might be a good topic for our first one, and when can we schedule it?

 Affirmation

What I appreciate most about the way you relate to our children is . . .

 Prayer

Father, we confess our inability to be and do all that our children need. Thank you for using others in the body of Christ to touch our children's lives. Above all, Lord, touch our children by Your Spirit. We pray that each of them will enjoy a close relationship with You . . .

WE, THE FAMILY

Visualizing the Future

In his challenging book, *Building Respect, Responsibility and Spiritual Values in Your Child*, Mike Phillips claims that "Vision is the key to successful parenting.... In faith begin to visualize your child as God sees him—at the pinnacle of maturity.... Regrettably, most parents are not daily setting imaginative goals and creating strategies for reaching them."[5]

Child Raising

This could be applied to the family as a whole. What kind of family do you want to have ten or fifteen years down the road?

 ## Bible Study

Read aloud Deuteronomy 6:1-9. What qualities did God desire in the Israelite family?

Ask yourselves: *What implications does that have for us? How can we be impressing God's Word on our children's hearts?*

Here are ideas to get you started:

— weekly family worship times (see bibliography)
— daily devotions (how and when?)
— memorizing one verse per week, at dinnertimes
— making a Scripture memory notebook
   (illustrated) with each child
— learn to turn everyday incidents into
   mini-lessons about God's working

(Record your thoughts and specific plans in your Talkbook.)

 ## Interaction

Let's discuss and write down the character qualities we would like to see God develop in our family. (If you've done chapter 10, you may already have some ideas in your Talkbook. Find a Scripture verse to claim for each quality if possible.)

Now do some dreaming for each child. After each one's name, write the kind of person you visualize him or her being at about age twenty-five. Leave several spaces between each one. (See the sample chart at the end of this chapter.)

Now for each child, ask: *What one character quality will we be praying that God will develop in his or her life over the next six months, which will move him toward the realization of that dream? How can we help this become a reality?*

Grabbing Hold of the Present

Recently Donna was at a hundred-year-old farmhouse in Switzerland, working on this book. She looked out the window one morning and saw the Swiss farmer and his wife turning over the newly-mown hay in the back orchard, to dry it in the sun. As they dug their pitchforks into the sweet-smelling grass, they talked and laughed with one another. As soon as the children returned from school, they also helped.

For that family, together-times are a natural part of every day. But we're being deceived if we think that, in our urbanized society, family togetherness will just happen. It takes willful, prayerful, careful planning to ensure that family members spend quality time in each other's presence every week.

One way that our family accomplishes this is through a weekly "family fun night." On these nights we do zany things like have puppet shows, make candles, dress up in costumes and play biblical charades. Attendance is required (although occasionally we have separate ones, because of the great age span between our children).

These nights are scheduled onto our calenders literally months in advance, although they can be rescheduled during the same week if need be.

 Interaction

Do we need family fun nights? If so, how often? Let's schedule the next few onto our calenders.

Now brainstorm. In your Talkbook, list fun night activities that your children might enjoy. They don't have to be only for evenings—you can include outings such as visiting a museum or playing miniature golf. Going to a movie or watching television don't count, because they do very little toward tightening the family bonds. (In this context, do you need to re-evaluate the use of television in your home?)

Affirmation

I am thankful for you and our children, and I value our relationships. I know we face obstacles, such as limited time and our own inadequacies, but I want us to strive together, in the power of the Holy Spirit, to build a godly family.

"Be strong and courageous....do not be discouraged, for the Lord your God will be with you wherever you go" (Joshua 1:9).

Child Raising

 Prayer

Thank You, Lord, for being with us. May we feel daily your presence in our home! Strengthen us to follow through on our ideas. Also, give us courage each day to trust our children and ourselves into Your care . . .

 Action Point

Let's review our discussion and set one simple goal. (For example: *We will pray daily for the next thirty days for the development of one character quality for each child.*)
(Record your goal and review it at your next retreat.)

CHILD VISION CHART

This chart can be used as a guide for comprehensive goalsetting and planning for your childrens' lives. Make a separate chart for each child. The chart should be revised every 6 months or so. Limit action plans to one per life area, and be ready to cut back further if child seems overwhelmed. (For small children, start with only one action plan per child per six months.)

In all my prayers for all of you, I always pray with joy...being confident of this, that He Who began a good work in you will carry it on to completion until the day of Christ Jesus." (Philippians 1:6)

Developmental Planning for _____
(Child's Name)

Life Areas	At Age 25 (Our Prayerful Goal)	Description of Present Reality	Focus of Prayer and Action Plan for Next 6 Mos.	Bible Promise to Claim
Spiritual:				
Mental:				
Physical:				
Social/ Emotional:				

Chapter 13
The Fruit That Won't Rot

One of our family's favorite Sunday activities is the "worship service" that takes place around the circle of couches and chairs in our living room. Because church ends early, we usually can squeeze this in between church and Sunday dinner. Everybody grabs a songbook and, whether or not they can read, each insists on having the book opened at the proper page.

Our all-time favorite song is "This Little Light of Mine," for which we all hold up one finger to represent a candle. And our children love most of all the line that runs, "Hide it under a bushel? NO! I'm gonna let it shine." They bellow out that NO! with a punch calculated to lift our duplex neighbors three feet into the air.

If only each of us had such forceful convictions about not hiding our light "under a bushel." Donna and I, even though we are "missionaries," know from our own experience what it is like to have, instead of convictions, a little pile of guilt-coated good intentions.

I sense that many Christian couples are retreating today, perhaps after some initial forays into the non-Christian world. Maybe they fear that too much exposure to the air of the "real" world will adversely affect their families, so they take cover in safe Christian circles.

Such apprehensions may be valid; on the other hand, a well-orchestrated attack is far more effective than a retreat. Besides, as German theologian Helmut Thielicke points out, when you take your light, crawl back under that bushel and pull it down over you, you quickly run out of air. "If he (the Christian) would only dare take Jesus' promise seriously and simply leap joyfully into life wherever he lives it, he would see that the light will not be blown out by the wind, but actually rekindled..."[1]

What promises of Jesus can guide us as we think about letting our light shine beyond the borders of our safe little marriage garden? Let's look at two:

> "You did not choose me, but I chose you to go and bear fruit—fruit that will last" (John 15:16).

Reaching Out

> But you will receive power when the Holy Spirit comes on you; and you will be my witnesses in Jerusalem, and in all Judea and Samaria, and to the ends of the earth (Acts 1:8).

From these two verses, it seems clear that:

1. "Witnessing" and "bearing fruit" are not optional in the Christian curriculum—Jesus considers them to be part of the normal Christian Life.
2. Jesus takes the initiative, He provides the power, and He will bring results. (See appendix C, *Have You Made the Wonderful Discovery of the Spirit-Filled Life?*)

In the area of West Germany where we live, practically every hill is covered with grapevines. They grow in neat rows, held in place by sturdy wires.

Sometimes, while walking through the woods, one also sees wild grapevines, which ramble any-old-which-way along a fence post. They certainly are "freer" than the bound-up cultivated vines. But their grapes, in contrast to the huge, sweet ones nurtured by the vinegrowers, are small and sour.

Some of us are settling for a "small and sour" version of the Christian life, because we have not been willing to be "bound up" by full obedience to Christ, especially regarding reaching out to others.

As best-selling author Rebecca Manley Pippert phrased it, "I don't see Jesus saying in the Bible, 'Go ye, therefore, all ye extroverts, all ye Scripture memory buffs, all of you with those dynamic relational skills...the rest of you can just sit around and sing some hymns; it's not your gift.' "[2]

152

Let's Begin Talking . . .

 Interaction

AN IMAGINARY STORY OF THE APOSTLE PAUL[3]

Imagine the following situation: Paul meets Jesus Christ and is saved on the Damascus road, as recorded in Acts 9. Although the Christians fear him at first, he eventually is accepted into the body of new believers in Jerusalem. Paul is thrilled with his new-found faith. He is encouraged by the friendship and fellowship of the local body of believers. Through the kindness of one of his new friends, Paul is offered a job as a tentmaker. For forty years Paul lives and works in Jerusalem at his trade. He becomes a respected Christian because of his knowledge of the Scriptures and matures to the point of leading a Bible study. He is faithful in attending worship services. Paul dies at age sixty-five in Jerusalem.

(Discuss your answers to the following and record ideas in your Talkbook.)

1. *What would have been the impact on the first-century church if this were Paul's real story?*
2. *How did Paul's life differ from the story we just read?* (Name three differences. His story is told in Acts 9-28.)
3. *In what specific ways has this exercise challenged our own thinking about reaching out?*

Reaching out to others essentially involves giving of yourselves; it's bringing the little that you have and holding it out in open hands before God and asking Him to take it and multiply it. Perhaps you shouldn't attempt to reach out if your marriage is presently on shaky ground, yet you can't wait until your home situation is "perfect" before you plunge in. Nothing is quite as refreshing to a stagnant marriage as when its two partners unite in stretching out their hands to others, in Christ's name!

In the following section, we'll discuss five facets of giving ourselves to others:

1. Giving our influence
2. Giving an account of our experience
3. Giving an explanation of the gospel
4. Giving help to those "on the way"
5. Giving our material resources

Reaching Out

Bible Study

(Answer the following questions based on the passages given.)

1. Why did Jesus come? (See John 4:31-36.)
2. What was the will of the Father concerning Jesus? (See Luke 19:10)
3. With what did Jesus charge His disciples in the so-called "Great Commission"? (See Matthew 28:19,20.)
4. If we say we "love the Lord," what is the indicator of that love? (See John 14:23,24.) How does our love for the Lord relate to reaching out to others?

Reaching Out

1. Giving Our Influence

> But thanks be to God, who always leads us in triumphal procession in Christ and through us spreads everywhere the fragrance of the knowledge of Him (2 Corinthians 2:14).

This verse encourages me, especially when I feel my personal "fragrance" is probably named "Stinker A-number-1." It tells me that God probably views "witnessing" in a much broader context than I tend to.

The influence of our lives begins in our "throne room." Are we in God's Word daily, letting it renew our thoughts? Are we praying for a mighty work of God's Spirit in the hearts of our non-Christian "neighbors" (i.e., people in our sphere of influence)?

Do we feel we have to be Mr. and Mrs. Perfect Christian, or are we free to share our human struggles, pointing to the only Perfect One? (If we were perfect, why would we need Jesus?) Do we invite non-Christians into our home and make them feel accepted and loved? Do we patiently bear with their children? Do we demonstrate genuine interest in them by asking questions and really listening to their answers?

"You know, you don't have to look for ways to evangelize. Life is evangelistic, if you're living life wanting Christ to be manifested in everything that you do...."[4]

 Interaction

Record ideas as you talk.

1. *Do we need to do more to cultivate friendships with non-Christians? How and with whom?*

2. *In what ways could we increase our hospitality to non-Christians?* (A neighborhood Christmas party, for example.)
3. *Let's talk about some areas in which we are experiencing struggles. How would we explain to non-Christian friends, without preaching or over-spiritualizing, the difference that Christ is making in the midst of these problems?*

2. Giving An Account Of Our Experience

> Always be prepared to give an answer to everyone who asks you to give the reason for the hope that you have (1 Peter 3:15).

A few months ago Donna invited one of our German neighbors in for coffee. In the course of their conversation, this working mother remarked to my wife, "You never yell at your kids. I don't want to either, but that's just the way I was raised and I can't seem to help it."

Donna took the opportunity to briefly tell the woman how she had come to faith in Christ. She was able to explain that, although she sometimes does yell at our children, Christ is enabling her to break some negative habit patterns. (The lines of communication are now even more open, and our neighbor has read two Christian books with great interest.)

Donna probably sounded quite spontaneous as she related how she had met the Lord. Several years ago, however, she took the time to write down her story, or "testimony," so that she would have it clearly in mind when a conversational opportunity arose.

The gospel changes lives, and people are naturally curious about that. After all, if God can change you, there's hope for them! So it is important to know how to share with others how God has worked in your life.

 Interaction

Each take a blank sheet and write down phrases that you would include as part of your individual story of how you met the Lord. Divide your paper into three sections:

1. *My life before knowing Christ.* (Be transparent, but don't share details that are in bad taste.)

2. *How I came to know Christ personally.* (Make this clear, so that your listener would understand how one can become a Christian.)
3. *My life after accepting Christ.* (Admit you still have imperfections, but what are some changes for the better?)

Before you begin to write, ask for the Holy Spirit's guidance. (Use the expanded outline in appendix B to help you organize your thoughts.)

Reaching Out

Discuss your preliminary ideas with each other. Listen with non-Christian ears and help each other weed out religious-sounding jargon. Remember, this is not a sermon, but an account of meeting the Lord and experiencing His work in your life.

Now take fresh sheets of paper and each write your testimony in a conversational style. Keep it brief enough to be spoken in about three minutes.

Read the results aloud to each other. Does it sound genuine? Interesting? Relevant to non-Christians? Refine until you have something you could say in conversation with a business associate or a mother down the street.

3. Giving An Explanation Of The Gospel

> And how can they believe in the one of whom they have not heard? And how can they hear without someone preaching to them? (Romans 10:14).

We talk about "loving people into the kingdom," and there's a lot of truth in that. Simply hitting them mechanically with words doesn't honor God (even though it may "work," because God uses His Word).

Yet there is a time for all things, and that includes a time to give a clear, concise presentation of the essence of the gospel to someone who is ready for it. "I am not ashamed of the gospel," wrote Paul, "because it is the power of God for the salvation of everyone who believes" (Romans 1:16).

Today Christendom probably has thousands of little booklets that can be read through with an interested seeker, or left behind after a conversation that touched on the spiritual. Some people frown on these booklets, saying they are too "canned," but I eat and enjoy many things that come out of cans, as long as they are cooked and served properly! Booklets such as the Four Spiritual

Laws, published by Campus for Crusade for Christ, are useful tools in making the main issues clear and in emphasizing exactly how one can put his faith in Christ as Savior.

Loaning Christian books to an interested person is another good way to present the gospel. Many books are written with the seeking non-Christian in mind. (See the bibliography for suggestions.)

Many churches offer evangelism courses, which are a great help in overcoming the initial inertia of witnessing. For information about personal evangelism seminars in your area, check with your pastor or write to:

Here's Life America
8213 Shoal Creek - Suite 105
Austin, TX 78758

Reaching Out

If you are carrying around a gospel booklet, how will you use it? You can't just whip it out when someone asks, "How's the weather?" On a recent flight to London, I wanted to share the gospel with the businessman next to me. I had spiritual lockjaw for about forty minutes, however, because I couldn't think of an appropriate question that could turn the conversation to Christ. (The Lord finally untied my tongue, and we had a great conversation about the differences between personal Christianity and "churchianity.")

The following questions can help peel the conversational onion and direct matters toward the spiritual:

A good sequence to use with acquaintances:

> *"What brings you the most satisfaction in life?"* (Or *"in your job?"*)
>
> *"We've never had a chance to chat about your religious back- ground. At what point are you in your spiritual pilgrim- age?"*
>
> *"Sometime I'd like to share with you four principles that have helped me understand what it means to establish a personal relationship with God."*

In a discussion about current events, world or national issues, etc.:

> *"What do you think is basically wrong with the world?"*
>
> *"Have you ever considered what Jesus Christ had to say about this"* (Refer to the Lord's diagnosis of man in Mark 7:21-23.)

After hearing someone describe a problem, frustration, concern, etc., with which you can identify:

> *"You know, I used to experience something quite similar until I discovered something that completely changed my outlook on _____ . Could I take a few minutes to tell you about what I found?"* (Share your testimony, then an outline of the gospel.)

Reaching Out

If your experience has not been similar to the one described by a non-Christian, you could say:

> *"You know, I probably would feel exactly the same way if not for an experience that changed my outlook on life."*

After even a vague reference to "religion" in a conversation, consider this series of questions:

> *"By the way, are you interested in spiritual things?"*
> *"What do you think a real Christian is?"*
> *"Would you be interested in knowing the Bible's explanation of a real Christian?"*

In response to a reference to God:

> *"What is your concept of God?"*
> *"Has anyone ever taken time to explain how you can know God personally?"*
> *"Would you mind if I shared something about that, which has been very helpful to me?"*

With someone having a strong religious background or interest in religion:

> *"I can tell that you've thought more than most people about spiritual things. How do you think a person becomes a Christian?"*
> *"I'd like to get your opinion of a booklet that I've found helpful to my own thinking. Have you ever heard of the Four Spiritual Laws?"*

With someone who relates God and religion to doing "good works":

"Suppose you died tonight and, as you stood before God, He asked you, 'Why should I let you into heaven?' What would you say?"

With someone who claims to be an atheist or agnostic:

"Do you think that God could exist outside your scope of knowledge?"
"If He does exist, how might He most effectively reveal Himself to mankind?" (Address the incarnation and deity of Christ.)

With someone who is turned off toward religion:

"A lot about religion turns me off, too! But I have discovered there's a big difference between religion and personal Christianity. And, frankly, that discovery has had a very positive effect on every area of my life. Could I tell you about what I discovered?"

 Interaction

Pretend you have invited a non-Christian couple you know to come over for dessert. Using some of the questions above (or better ones you think of), have a conversation, with the two of you playing the four parts. (One of you play the Christian couple and one the non-Christian. Pitch your voice higher or lower to play "wife" or "husband.") Try to actually get the conversation to the point of explaining the gospel.

Of course, in real life it won't go exactly as you plan it, yet it's encouraging to see that you can share the gospel with others!

4. Giving Help To New Believers

We proclaim Him, admonishing and teaching everyone with all wisdom, so that we may present everyone perfect in Christ (Colossians 1:28).

We all know people "on the way." Some are on the way to discovering a relationship with Christ. They aren't there yet, but they are open and interested. All they need is some time to think about the facts and to observe Christ's people up close.

Others in our circle of influence may have put their trust in Christ recently and are setting out on the way to knowing Him better. They need love, encouragement and instruction in the basics of Christian faith.

Still others are further along the way to a deeper walk with the Lord, but they seek to meet with other believers for in-depth Bible study, the bond of fellowship through prayer, and motivation to witness.

Reaching Out

Finally, some Christian couples are on the way to a closer, more enriching relationship with each other. They would benefit from meeting with other couples and discussing together a book or tapes on Christian marriage. Guidelines for using this book with a Marriage Growth Group are found in appendix D.

You also are traveling "on the way," and probably have friends in most of these four groups. One very productive method for you, as a couple, to reach out to others is to open your home as a meeting place for one or more groups.

Perhaps your throat is getting dry and your heart beating faster as you read this. You may be asking, "Does this mean that we would have to (gulp) teach the group?"

Not at all. Hosting a group doesn't necessarily involve leading it. You might know of several mature Christians in your church who would be willing to lead a group meeting in your home. You could function as the initiators, the ones who draw the group members together and get them motivated.

Yet, I'd like to encourage you to also consider guiding the group yourselves, instead of bringing in someone else. You don't have to know more than the other group members. See the bibliography for materials that contain instructions for forming groups and guiding discussions. Many study booklets allow groups to discover and apply spiritual truth themselves, once the leader knows a few principles of group dynamics.

 Interaction

Brainstorm about the possibility of starting a group in your home. Record ideas in your Talkbook.

Considering our circle of acquaintances, which of these would we be more interested in?
1. A discovery group (for not-yet-Christians)

2. *A growth group (for those young in faith)*
3. *A Bible study group (for mature believers)*
4. *A marriage enrichment group*
5. *Or, some other type of group not mentioned here*

Let's discuss the details of getting a group started:

1. *Who should we include on our tentative list of group members?* (A total of eight to ten people is maximum for good discussion.)
2. *How often should the group meet? When? For how many weeks?* (People will be more willing to commit to a group that lasts a specific number of weeks—say five to eight.) *When should we begin?*
3. *How should we get the word out about the group? What is the most appealing way we can phrase our invitation?*
4. *Let's make necessary notes on our calendars to get the process started.*

5. Giving Our Material Resources

Give, and it will be given to you. A good measure, pressed down, shaken together and running over, will be poured into your lap (Luke 6:38).

In his book *Your Finances in Changing Times*, Christian financial counselor Larry Burkett writes:

God's freedom cannot be experienced in the area of finances unless one:
A. acknowledges God's ownership over everything and accepts the role of a steward;
B. surrenders the first part back to God;
C. seeks the reason that God supplies him a surplus above his own basic needs."[5]

These concepts are developed more fully in Burkett's book and workbook, *How to Manage Your Money* (which, by the way, is excellent for couples wanting to think through all aspects of their finances). For our purposes here, I'll assume you generally agree with the above statements.(If not, I refer you to chapter II of this book.)

If so, the question is not, "Should we give?" but rather, "To whom should we give?" You naturally will want to share your "wealth" with the local church where you are fed and nurtured. In some cases, you may want to take a more vocal part in urging that the church monies are directed outward to missions, as well as inward.

But many Christian organizations also operate on the basis of donations. "Many are deserving," says Burkett, "but some are poorly managed, unfruitful, even dishonest. Seek God's wisdom before giving. Get literature....talk to others....be discerning."[6]

Reaching Out

 ## Interaction

Ask the Lord for wisdom and unity of mind before proceeding. *Do we need to increase our giving? By what amount? What individuals or organizations would we like to investigate as possible recipients? Let's plan how we will go about checking them out.*

 ## Affirmation

"And God is able to make all grace abound to you, so that in all things at all times, having all that you need, you will abound in every good work" (2 Corinthians 9:8).

 ## Prayer

Lord, we acknowledge that You are far more interested in our availability than our ability. We want to give what we have and who we are to help further Your kingdom. Thank You for the assurance that You have commissioned us to go and bear lasting fruit. Take these plans we have made, give us boldness to follow through, and go before us to prepare hearts to listen and respond.

 ## Action Point

Let's review our discussions and set one simple goal. (For example: We will write out a "Ten Most Wanted" list with the names of ten friends and relatives that we desire to see come into eternal relationships with Jesus Christ. We will pray regularly that God would draw them to faith. Also, we will ask the Lord for wisdom to know how to "put feet to our prayers.")

(Record your goal here and review it often.)

Back to Reality

Chapter 14

Subdue
Those Weekly Weeds

The two of you have spent the last few hours or days engaged in some strenuous marriage "gardening." You probably got your hands dirty and did some emotional sweating in the process. I trust that you also have experienced the sense of accomplishment that comes from intense marital spadework.

But don't quit now—your task has only just begun! If you don't take time to tackle the weeds that surely will spring up, your marriage retreat's good effects will be greatly diminished.

This chapter will give you three "how-to's" for subduing those weekly weeds:

— how to live with unresolved tensions
— how to wrap up your retreat, and
— how to establish regular talk times.

LIVING WITH UNRESOLVED TENSIONS

Residing overseas for the past four years has taught us a few things about our homeland. One insight we've gained is that, compared to many other peoples throughout the world, we Americans have a very low tolerance for unresolved issues.

When an American sees a problem, he doesn't ask himself, "Will I try to solve this?" Of course he'll try! His only question is, "How can I solve it quickly and effectively?"

That's one reason for this book—to assist in problem-solving in marriage. But realistically, some tensions cannot be dissolved through a few intense discussions. Certain ones may disappear only after many years. Others may never go away.

What do you do when tensions remain between you as a couple or within your family, for which there is no hope of resolution? How do you face the prospect of year after year of conflict

over a certain issue? Maybe it is
- a negative trait of your mate;
- a difficult child;
- a hard-to-love relative;
- the pressures of your career;
- disagreement over a major issue, like child raising.

How should you respond? The following are three suggestions.

Love by Faith

First, let the concept of a "faith marriage" sink deeply into your garden soil. Just as you became a Christian by faith, and grow by faith (see Philippians 1:6), so also you live as Christian partners by faith. Having a faith marriage means accepting your mate as being handed to you by God. Do you experience tensions? Probably so. Does your partner have negative traits that will not change? Absolutely!

The Lord is aware of these, and He intends to use them constructively.

> And we know that in all things God works for the good of those who love Him, who have been called according to His purpose.... to be conformed to the likeness of His Son (Romans 8:28-29).

Each of you is like a diamond-cutting tool in the hand of God, as He fashions the other into the image of His Son. Moreover, if all of our marital problems were solved, it's unlikely that we would pray much for our marriages. Unresolved negatives keep us on our knees.

Even in a very good marriage, partners do not always feel tender and romantic toward each other. That's when it's time to *love by faith.*

> Faith is like the starter of a car — it starts the powerful motor which drives the vehicle. Faith releases the limitless power of God in a situation.[1]

Loving by faith means turning to God to ask Him to give us His love for another person. In the Transferable Concept *How to*

166

Love by Faith, Bill Bright gives the following steps:

a. See that God is the source of unconditional love (Romans 5:8, John 17:23, 1 John 4:19).
b. Realize that God's love lives within us, because the Holy Spirit lives within us (John 17:26, Romans 5:5).
c. By faith, claim God's love for the other person. We know that God wants us to love— He commanded it. By faith, we trust God to give us His unending supply of agape love for our family members. This applies also for people in our churches whom we don't like! We cannot love such people in our own strength; we must receive the love from God.[2]

As we learn to let God be the source for our marital love, much of the stress of unresolved tensions will be siphoned away.

Bend Before You Break

Second, ask God for wisdom on how to bend.

> If any of you lacks wisdom, he should ask God, who gives generously to all without finding fault, and it will be given to him. (James 1:5).

Consider the following potential conflict situations:
— Husband manages the family finances. Wife is sure she could do a much better job, but he won't give her a chance.
— Husband believes in spanking kids hard. Wife isn't sure what she believes and can't bring herself to do it.
— Wife wants to transfer the kids to a Christian school. Husband wants to stick it out with the public school.

What do you do when you disagree on a major issue? One or both must bend before you break. Bending is not the sole responsibility of either partner; 1 Peter 3:1-8 gives counsel for both (the words are taken directly from the New International Version):

To wives:
— be submissive
— [demonstrate] purity and reverence

— adornment.... [to be] of your inner self.
— [have] a gentle and quiet spirit

To husbands:
— be considerate
— treat wives with respect
— treat them... as heirs with you of the gracious gift of life

To both:
— live in harmony with one another
— be sympathetic
— love as brothers
— be compassionate and humble

Wrap-Up

The Lord will give wisdom for each situation as both partners are willing to yield to each other and to Him. Let Him help you remain flexible—a brittle cookie is most likely to crumble!

Minimize the Effects

A third suggestion for living with unresolved conflicts is, if you can't change a negative issue, at least *take action to minimize its negative effects*. One step in this direction is to understand the ways in which you respond to tension.

Donna and I tend to respond to pressure in the same way: we become overly perfectionistic. I start noticing every speck of dirt in the house. She suddenly sees with brilliant clarity every character flaw in me and our children. (The Lord knew what He was doing when He gave us three wacky, over-confident kids! If they'd been the least bit quiet or sensitive, we probably would have squashed their personalities by now.)

How do you react to tension? Take a few minutes to identify yourselves on the following list:

nag	complain
pout	explode
criticize	become cool, silent
withhold sex	ignore the problem
stay away from home	talk negatively about him/her
become perfectionistic	to other family members

When we recognize how we tend to react under pressure, can make it a matter of prayer. Donna and I have agreed to remind each other when the pressure-response kicks on. Even though we can't always stop our reactions, just realizing what's happening often relieves a lot of the stress.

To review, living with unresolved issues involves:
— loving by faith;
— bending so you won't break; and
— minimizing negative effects.

RETREAT WRAP-UP

Keeping in mind that you can't tie up every loose end into a neat bundle, take some time now to bring your marriage retreat to a close.

You've talked and talked *and talked,* probably about a wide variety of subjects. You may have come up with a hundred ideas for how you want your lives to be different, starting right now. Can you put all of these ideas into practice? No way!

Funnel It Down

Does that mean that frustration is the inevitable last stop on the line? Not necessarily. Instead of throwing up your hands in frustration, *funnel* your retreat ideas into a workable container.

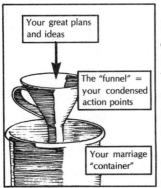

Your marriage "container" can only hold so much at one time. It probably does not have the capacity for all the ideas you recorded in your loose-leaf Talkbook. So look back and see what you wrote at the end of each chapter under "Let's set one simple goal." These become your "Action Points."

What is an action point? It is something that you intend to do to initiate change in a certain area of your life. The following are some examples of action points:

— pray for your four-year-old to develop more self-control
— read a book on child discipline
— begin having a quiet time for fifteen minutes each morning
— sign up for an aerobics class
— invite Sunday school teacher and his wife over for dinner
— schedule a monthly "date night" with spouse
— begin consciously hugging each child once a day
— request transfer to another department at work

Wrap-Up

You may want to revise or add to the action points that you wrote. For the sake of simplicity, however, I suggest that you streamline your many possible action points into two for each of you individually, two that involve both of you together and one for each child. (Children get very discouraged if we try to change everything about them at once. Six months later you can tackle something else.)

Frustration diminishes as you go on *regular* marriage retreats (ideally one every six months). You won't worry as much about not being able immediately to assimilate all your ideas, when you realize that six months later you'll have another chance. Anne Ortlund says that she and her pastor husband Ray go out of town one day a month to pray, think and evaluate progress toward their goals.

 Interaction

You also have left many topics untouched during your retreat time. Therefore, before you write down your action points, take time to talk briefly through the following:

Are there actions we need to take in the following areas?
1. *Physical* (diet, exercise, visit doctor, etc.)
2. *Spiritual* (quiet time, prayer, join Bible study group, etc.)
3. *Social* (more time together, join a club, hospitality, etc.)
4. *Parental* (expressing more consistent love/discipline, etc.)
5. *Vocational* (pursue change of job or working conditions, etc.)
6. *Financial* (increase giving, savings plan, begin a budget, etc.)
7. *Outreach* (get training in sharing our faith, start a prayer group, teach a Sunday school class, etc.)

Use the above to glean a few possible action points. Again,

don't go overboard—just pick the ones of greatest need at the present. Review your Talkbook and check off the ideas that you consider most vital. Two action points apiece and two to work on together, along with one for each child, are enough to start with.

Now take a sheet from your Talkbook and head it Retreat Wrap-Up, (date). See appendix A for a sample Retreat Wrap-up sheet.

 Action Point

It may be tough to funnel your action points down to so few. If you want to try for three each, go for it—but don't say I didn't warn you! Write them in your Talkbook.

The next step is to schedule your action points onto your calendars. This helps make sure that they'll really get done! (This process is outlined in more detail in chapter 10.)

While you have your calendar in front of you, schedule your next marriage retreat!

Become Accountable

Even with this careful planning, putting your ideas into action is sometimes near-impossible. You may open the door back home to discover your house is a wreck, the kids haven't changed a bit, and neither have you! It's tempting to give up before you start.

Don't do it! Remember that the Lord is in the business of making you like Christ, in His way and in His time. He's not giving up!

One thing that Donna and I have found helpful in seeing ideas become reality is *accountability*. This involves finding another person or couple and asking them if you can be accountable to them to make sure you complete what you've set out to do. This person (or couple) would:

— commit to pray for you in this area
— call you regularly to ask how you're progressing
— be encouraged to be firm with you if your commitment wanes

As mates you can also be accountable to each other. Donna has asked me to remind her to exercise daily. I appreciate her asking me if I've had my quiet time. This means we've got to sustain a grace relationship and not succumb to nagging.

If you're really serious about wanting to change, it's best to enlist the aid of a third party. Band together with another couple, or even with a group of couples, and determine to become accountable to each other.

ESTABLISH REGULAR TALK TIMES

Wrap-Up

What's the best way to ensure that the benefits of a good marriage retreat continue? Establish regular times to interact genuinely with one another, evaluate your progress thus far and determine to press on.

Without a regular talk time, you probably won't be able to follow through on your action points. A new baby, a job change, a move, a death in the family—any one of these brings great upheaval. Many lesser things also can move around the dirt in the marriage garden! At times we don't even remember whether we *had* a retreat in the last six months, still less what we discussed.

I recommend that you set aside time every week for in-depth talking. Once a month should be the absolute minimum. Schedule the time onto your calendar, and pick a quiet place where you won't be interrupted.

For your first talk time, consider making a date to re-read chapter 3 of this book and use the questions for week 5 in appendix D as a springboard for interaction.

How can you make sure you use a regular talk time to its fullest? (Incidentally, these same ideas apply to taking marriage retreats after you've worked through every chapter in this book.)

1. *Write down important issues* as they occur to either of you in your loose-leaf Talkbook. Keep the Talkbook in a permanent, handy place, like on a bedside table, so that you can record questions or ideas as they come to mind. Take your Talkbook with you on each talk time, to discuss what you've written and add new ideas.

2. *Review and evaluate progress* based on your previous marriage retreat. Since your action plans are recorded on one page, you easily can read over them and ask, "Are we doing that? If not, why not? Should we forget it, or keep at it?" (This retreat evaluation is necessary only about once a month.)

3. *Draw each other out.* Learn to probe beneath the surface,

to discover the hidden depths of the person you married. The bibliography for chapter 14 lists several books that contain questions. A couple we know uses the following list of questions in their regular talk times.

1. *How has your week been going?*
2. *Is there anything that I can be praying for you about? Are you praying for me?*
3. *What have you been learning from the Lord?*
4. *How is your relationship with your immediate supervisor?*
5. *Who should we have over for dinner or dessert?*
6. *Have you become aware of or crossed any faith barriers?*
7. *What did you most enjoy doing this week?*
8. *How do you feel about our relationship?*
9. *How is our sex life?*
10. *Have I done or said anything this week, publicly or privately, that upset you or made you angry?*
11. *Have I done or said anything this week that you particularly appreciated?*
12. *Is there anything that I can help you with?*
13. *Do you know that I love you?*

These are simply ideas to get you going; design your own questions to suit your unique relationship.

Handling a Hot Topic

Don't be afraid to be real with each other in your talk times. Conflict is normal in marriage! It can be quite healthy, if couples learn to handle inflammatory topics without getting burned.

If you have an issue that's too hot to handle, try working through the steps on the accompanying chart.

The last step, by the way, is the surest way to cool down an overheated subject—pour a little honest prayer over it! And it doesn't hurt a bit to check to see if self or the Holy Spirit is at the controls.

Wrap-Up

Handling A Hot Topic

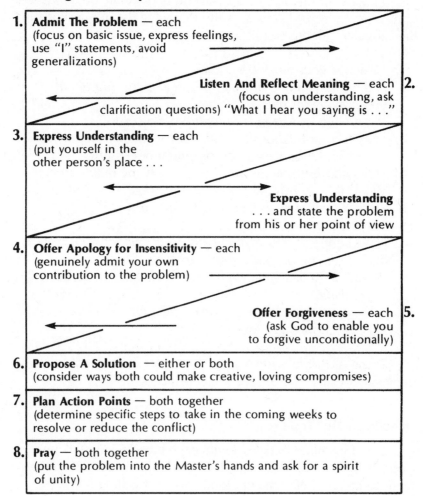

1. **Admit The Problem** — each
(focus on basic issue, express feelings, use "I" statements, avoid generalizations)

Listen And Reflect Meaning — each **2.**
(focus on understanding, ask clarification questions) "What I hear you saying is . . ."

3. **Express Understanding** — each
(put yourself in the other person's place . . .

Express Understanding
. . . and state the problem from his or her point of view

4. **Offer Apology for Insensitivity** — each
(genuinely admit your own contribution to the problem)

Offer Forgiveness — each **5.**
(ask God to enable you to forgive unconditionally)

6. **Propose A Solution** — either or both
(consider ways both could make creative, loving compromises)

7. **Plan Action Points** — both together
(determine specific steps to take in the coming weeks to resolve or reduce the conflict)

8. **Pray** — both together
(put the problem into the Master's hands and ask for a spirit of unity)

Back to Reality

It's checkout time—marriage retreat checkout, that is. Time to head home to laundry and cooking and doctor's appointments and deadlines and the jarring realities of life with children. Will your retreat euphoria last? Nope. It's guaranteed to evaporate about ten minutes after you open your front door. Will the benefits last? I believe so, if you pursue the guidelines given in this chapter.

I can overhear the neighbors talking, a few years down the road:

"Just look at that lettuce! And did you see the size of those tomatoes?"

"No—I was too busy noticing the flowers. I've never seen any so bright and fresh!"

"I agree—and what a lovely garden wall!"

That's your marriage garden they're talking about—well-cultivated, flourishing, a delight to the eye and a real credit to the Master Gardener.

Happy hoeing!

Wrap-Up

Retreat Wrap-Up Worksheet

Appendix A

Follow-through Notes for Marriage Growth

Retreat date(s) _____ Location _____

ACTION POINTS

Husband: 1. _____
_____

2. _____
_____

Wife: 1. _____
_____

2. _____
_____

Together: 1. _____
_____

2. _____
_____

Children: (One per child) 1. _____
_____

2. _____
_____

3. _____
_____

Testimony Worksheet

Appendix B

How To Relate Your Christian Experiences Effectively

(If you became a Christian as a child, build your testimony around the ideas shown in parentheses.)

1. What was your life like before you put your faith in Jesus Christ (or totally committed your life to Him)?
   a. What were your attitudes, needs, problems?
   b. What did your life revolve around? What was most important to you?
   c. What did you look to for security, peace of mind, happiness? In what ways did you find activities unsatisfying?

2. What led to your decision to trust Christ? (How did you come to give Him complete control of your life?)
   a. When did you first hear and understand the gospel? How? (When were you first exposed to dynamic Christianity?)
   b. What were your initial reactions to the message?
   c. When and why did you begin to feel positive toward Christianity?
   d. Exactly how did you receive Christ? What did you say or pray?

3. What happened after you trusted Christ (or gave Him complete control of your life)?
   a. What changes did you see in your life: actions, attitudes, problems? Use specific examples. If possible, talk about changes that correspond to the needs or problems you

expressed in the first part of your testimony.
  b. How long did it take you to notice changes?
  c. Conclusion: What does Jesus Christ mean to you now?

A few important tips:

1. Avoid mentioning denominations or making statements that reflect negatively on church, other people or organizations.
2. Don't use words like "joyful," "happy," or "changed" without explaining them.
3. Avoid using biblical words such as "saved," "born again," "converted" and "sin" without clarifying what you mean.
4. Give enough details to arouse interest, but keep the total length to no more than three to four minutes.
5. Use one or (at the most) two Scripture references only if they relate directly to your experience and fit in naturally.
6. Avoid "preaching." Speak of personal experiences to which people can easily relate. (Let the Holy Spirit do the convincing.)

Have You Made the Wonderful Discovery of the Spirit-Filled Life?

Every day can be an exciting adventure for the Christian who knows the reality of being filled with the Holy Spirit and who lives constantly, moment by moment, under His gracious direction.

The Bible tells us that there are three kinds of people:

NATURAL MAN (one who has not received Christ).

But a natural man does not accept the things of the Spirit of God; for they are foolishness to him, and he cannot understand them, because they are spiritually appraised (1 Corinthians 2:14).

SELF-DIRECTED LIFE
S—Self is on the throne
†—Christ is outside the life
●—Interests are directed by self, often resulting in discord and frustration

SPIRITUAL MAN (one who is directed and empowered by the Holy Spirit).

But he who is spiritual appraises all things . . . (1 Corinthians 2:15).

CHRIST-DIRECTED LIFE
†—Christ is in the life and on the throne
S—Self is yielding to Christ
●—Interests are directed by Christ, resulting in harmony with God's plan

CARNAL MAN (one who has received Christ, but who lives in defeat because he trusts in his own efforts to live the Christian life).

> And I, brethren, could not speak to you as to spiritual men, but as to carnal men, as to babes in Christ. I gave you milk to drink, not solid food; for you were not yet able to receive it. Indeed, even now you are not yet able, for you are still carnal. For since there is jealousy and strife among you, are you not fleshly, and are you not walking like mere men? (1 Corinthians 3:1-3).

Appendix C

SELF-DIRECTED LIFE
S—Self is on the throne
†—Christ dethroned and not allowed to direct the life
●—Interests are directed by self, often resulting in discord and frustration

Three key truths introduce God's provision, His requirement and His promise for the Spirit-filled life.

1 God has provided for us an abundant and fruitful Christian life.

Jesus said, "I came that they might have life, and might have it abundantly" (John 10:10).

I am the vine, you are the branches; he who abides in Me, and I in him, he bears much fruit; for apart from Me you can do nothing (John 15:5).

But the fruit of the Spirit is love, joy, peace, patience, kindness, goodness, faithfulness, gentleness, self-control; against such things there is no law (Galatians 5:22,23).

But you shall receive power when the Holy Spirit has come upon you; and you shall be My witnesses both in Jerusalem, and in all Judea and Samaria, and even to the remotest part of the earth (Acts 1:8).

THE SPIRITUAL MAN—Some personal traits which result from trusting God:

Christ-centered
Empowered by the Holy Spirit
Introduces others to Christ
Effective prayer life
Understands God's Word
Trusts God
Obeys God

Love
Joy
Peace
Patience
Kindness
Faithfulness
Goodness

The degree to which these traits are manifested in the life depends upon the extent to which the Christian trusts the Lord with every detail of his life, and upon his maturity in Christ. One who is only beginning to understand the ministry of the Holy Spirit should not be discouraged if he is not as fruitful as the more mature Christians who have known and experienced this truth for a longer period.

Why is it that most Christians are not experiencing the abundant life?

2 Carnal Christians cannot experience the abundant and fruitful Christian life.

The carnal man trusts in his own efforts to live the Christian life:

A. He is either uninformed about, or has forgotten, God's love, forgiveness, and power (Romans 5:8-10; Hebrews 10:1-25; 1 John 1; 2:1-3; 2 Peter 1:9; Acts 1:8).
B. He has an up-and-down spiritual experience.
C. He cannot understand himself—he wants to do what is right, but cannot.
D. He fails to draw upon the power of the Holy Spirit to live the Christian life (1 Corinthians 3:1-3; Romans 7:15-24; 8:7; Galatians 5:16-18).

THE CARNAL MAN—Some or all of the following traits may characterize the Christian who does not fully trust God:

Ignorance of his spiritual heritage
Unbelief
Disobedience
Loss of love for God and for others
Poor prayer life
No desire for Bible study
Legalistic attitude

Impure thoughts
Jealousy
Guilt
Worry
Discouragement
Critical spirit
Frustration
Aimlessness

(The individual who professes to be a Christian but who continues to practice sin should realize that he may not be a Christian at all, according to 1 John 2:3; 3:6,9; Ephesians 5:5).

The third truth gives us the only solution to this problem . . .

3 Jesus promised the abundant and fruitful life as the result of being filled (directed and empowered) by the Holy Spirit.

The Spirit-filled life is the Christ-directed life by which Christ lives His life in and through us in the power of the Holy Spirit (John 15).

A. One becomes a Christian through the ministry of the Holy Spirit, according to John 3:1-8. From the moment of spiritual birth, the Christian is indwelt by the Holy Spirit at all times (John 1:12; Colossians 2:9,10; John 14:16,17). *Though all Christians are indwelt by the Holy Spirit, not all Christians are filled (directed and empowered) by the Holy Spirit.*

B. The Holy Spirit is the source of the overflowing life (John 7:37-39).

C. The Holy Spirit came to glorify Christ (John 16:1-15). When one is filled with the Holy Spirit, he is a true disciple of Christ.

D. In His last command before His ascension, Christ promised the power of the Holy Spirit to enable us to be witnesses for Him (Acts 1:1-9).

Appendix C

How, then, can one be filled with the Holy Spirit?

We are filled (directed and empowered) by the Holy Spirit by faith; then we can experience the abundant and fruitful life which Christ promised to each Christian.

You can appropriate the filling of the Holy Spirit *right now* if you:

A. Sincerely desire to be directed and empowered by the Holy Spirit (Matthew 5:6; John 7:37-39).

B. Confess your sins.
By *faith* thank God that He *has* forgiven all of your sins—past, present and future—because Christ died for you (Colossians 2:13-15; 1 John 1; 2:1-3; Hebrews 10:1-17).

C. Present every area of your life to God (Romans 12:1,2).

D. By *faith* claim the fullness of the Holy Spirit, according to:
1. HIS COMMAND—Be filled with the Spirit. "And do not get drunk with wine, for that is dissipation, but be filled with the Spirit" (Ephesians 5:18).
2. HIS PROMISE—He will always answer when we pray according to His will. "And this is the confidence which we have before Him, that, if we ask anything according to His will, He hears us. And if we know that He hears us in whatever we ask, we know that we have the requests which we have asked from Him" (1 John 5:14,15).

Faith can be expressed through prayer . . .

How to pray in faith to be filled with the Holy Spirit

We are filled with the Holy Spirit by *faith* alone. However, true prayer is one way of expressing your faith. The following is a suggested prayer.

> "Dear Father, I need You. I acknowledge that I have been directing my own life and that, as a result, I have sinned against You. I thank You that You have forgiven my sins through Christ's death on the cross for me. I now invite Christ to take His place again on the throne of my life. Fill me with the Holy Spirit as You *commanded* me to be filled, and as You *promised* in Your Word that You would do if I asked in faith. I pray this in the name of Jesus. As an expression of my faith, I now thank You for directing my life and for filling me with the Holy Spirit."

Does this prayer express the desire of your heart? If so, bow in prayer and trust God to fill you with the Holy Spirit *right now.*

How to know that you are filled (directed and empowered) by the Holy Spirit

Did you ask God to fill you with the Holy Spirit? Do you know that you are now filled with the Holy Spirit? On what authority? (On the trustworthiness of God Himself and His Word: Hebrews 11:6; Romans 14:22,23).

Do not depend upon feelings. The promise of God's Word, not our feelings, is our authority. The Christian lives by faith (trust) in the trustworthiness of God Himself and His Word. This train diagram illustrates the relationship between *fact* (God and His Word), *faith* (our trust in God and His Word), and *feeling* (the result of our faith and obedience) (John 14:21).

The train will run with or without the caboose. However, it would be futile to attempt to pull the train by the caboose. In the same way, we, as Christians, do not depend upon feelings or emotions, but we place our faith (trust) in the trustworthiness of God and the promises of His Word.

How to walk in the Spirit

Faith (trust in God and in His promises) is the only means by which a Christian can live the Spirit-directed life. As you continue to trust Christ moment by moment:

A. Your life will demonstrate more and more of the fruit of the Spirit (Galatians 5:22,23) and will be more and more conformed to the image of Christ (Romans 12:2; 2 Corinthians 3:18).

B. Your prayer life and study of God's Word will become more meaningful.

C. You will experience His power in witnessing (Acts 1:8).

D. You will be prepared for spiritual conflict against the world (1 John 2:15-17); against the flesh (Galatians 5:16,17); and against Satan (1 Peter 5:7-9; Ephesians 6:10-13).

E. You will experience His power to resist temptation and sin (1 Corinthians 10:13; Philippians 4:13; Ephesians 1:19-23; 6:10; 2 Timothy 1:7; Romans 6:1-16).

Spiritual breathing

By faith you can continue to experience God's love and forgiveness. If you become aware of an area of your life (an attitude or an action) that is displeasing to the Lord, even though you are walking with Him and sincerely desiring to serve Him, simply thank God that He has forgiven your sins—past, present and future—on the basis of Christ's death on the cross. Claim His love and forgiveness by faith and continue to have fellowship with Him.

If you retake the throne of your life through sin—a definite act of disobedience—breathe spiritually.

Spiritual breathing (exhaling the impure and inhaling the pure) is an exercise in faith that enables you to continue to experience God's love and forgiveness.

1. *Exhale*—confess your sin. Agree with God concerning your sin and thank Him for His forgiveness of it, according to 1 John 1:9 and Hebrews 10:1-25. Confession involves repentance—a change in attitude and action.

2. *Inhale*—surrender the control of your life to Christ, and appropriate (receive) the fullness of the Holy Spirit by faith. Trust that He now directs and empowers you, according to the *command* of Ephesians 5:18, and the *promise* of 1 John 5:14,15.

Marriage Growth Group Guide

Appendix D

This book also can serve as a catalyst and guide for Marriage Growth Groups. For some, a two-day retreat might be too big a hurdle to jump without getting a "running start." The guidelines given below show how you can help get couples moving in the right direction through group interaction.

By using some of the workbook chapters as a basis for small group discussions, partners can develop an atmosphere of greater understanding and open communication. Hearing from others who are experiencing similar struggles and challenges in growing a Christian marriage can prove tremendously encouraging.

The suggestions given below are designed to enable initial group interaction to lead to more fruitful dialogue for each couple. Both group interaction and private couple dialogue can take place during the meeting. These exchanges should spark further communication at home during the days that follow.

Suggestions for starting a Marriage Growth Group:

1. Find three to five couples (maximum total of six couples) who would like to join you in a six-week experiment in marriage growth. (A short, definite timetable is more appealing than something open-ended and vague.)

2. Show them the book (especially the table of contents, pointing out topics being considered, and the layout of a typical chapter) and explain how the evening would be structured.

3. Select one night per week when all can gather for approximately two hours. Choose a home with enough rooms where each couple can discuss some of the questions with a degree of privacy.

4. Encourage each couple to buy the book and read chapters 1 and 2 before the first group meeting. They also should bring a small loose-leaf notebook to use as their "Talkbook" for the six weeks.

Appendix D   Note: To help other couples see the need for participating in a Marriage Growth Group, rent the film by Charles Swindoll, "Strike the Original Match," and show it to a larger group of couples in your church (Sunday school class, etc.). Organize one or more groups based upon interest shown.

Overview of the six-week program:

Week 1 — Chapter 6—Open Your Cans of Worms
            Developing no-barriers communication.

Week 2 — Chapter 8—"You Get the Shovel, I'll Take the Rake" (first half)
            Understanding and appreciating each other.

Week 3 — Chapter 8—"You Get the Shovel, I'll Take the Rake" (second half)
            Understanding and appreciating each other.

            (Group decides after week 3 which of the following they would prefer to cover in week 4.)

Week 4 — Chapter 12—Nurturing Your Young Olive Plants
            Helping your children grow into maturity.
            Or
            Chapter 7—Mortar in Your Garden Wall
            Tracking the elusive "spiritual oneness."

Week 5 — Chapter 3—Test Your Marriage Soil
            Three essential nutrients for a healthy garden.

Week 6 — Wrap-up meeting (possibly as a " pot-luck " dinner).

Format for weeks 1, 2, 3 and 4

15 min. Refreshments and general sharing.

5-10 min. Select someone to read opening text of chapter (down to the "Let's Begin Talking" exercise).

10-15 min. Do first Bible study exercise together as a group. (Possibly add next Bible study exercise if time permits.)

10-15 min. Select one or two questions from the "Let's Begin Talking" exercise or the first "Interaction" section and conduct a group discussion. (Choose questions that are appropriate for public interaction and can help launch each couple into further private interaction.)

45-50 min. Divide up as couples, each going to a different room, to continue reading and responding as indicated through the remainder of the chapter. Stress the importance of thorough communication instead of rushing to complete entire chapter. (Attempt to cover no more than half of chapter 8 per meeting.)

20 min. Reconvene the group for an "Anonymous Question Panel." (Distribute index cards and pencils. Encourage each person to write out a question to which they want others to respond. Folded cards and pencils are returned to the "moderator." He prioritizes the questions, reads, and invites group response to as many as time allows. Moderator then destroys all cards so that identity of questioners is protected.)

5 min. Encourage couples to complete the remainder of their chapter discussion during the week. Close in prayer, focusing on the Lordship of Christ over the area of marriage discussed that evening.

Appendix D

Appendix D

Format for week 5:

(Assign the Spirit-Filled Life—appendix C—to be read ahead of time.)

15 min. Refreshments and general sharing.

45 min. Group discussion of first five questions:
Read "First Nutrient: GRACE" silently; then discuss:

1. What kinds of feelings and responses do you experience when your partner relates to you in grace?
2. In what ways has "the Phantom" struck in your marriage relationship?

Read "Second Nutrient: COMMITMENT" silently; then discuss:

3. What relationship does your wedding vow have to a life-long commitment to each other? (Refer back to a "A Binding Contract" sub-section.)

Read "Third Nutrient: THE HOLY SPIRIT" silently: then discuss:

4. How can you be sure the Holy Spirit is present in your relationship?
5. If both partners are "filled with the Spirit," what affect will that have on the marriage relationship? (Refer to appendix C for insights.)

35 min. Divide up as couples, each going to a different room, and discuss the following five questions privately:

6. What are some examples of the "performance standard" which you have observed in your own marriage?
7. Discuss the fountain illustration. What application does it have to your marriage relationship?
8. What are some tangible ways in which you can express your commitment to one another?
9. What is usually the first indication that you are not being controlled by the Holy Spirit, but are

depending upon your own efforts to make the marriage work? (Partners answer for themselves.)

10. In what ways do you (as a couple) need to get back to the "basics" — grace, commitment, and the Spirit-led life?

Format for week 6:

During pot-luck dinner
— General sharing on what has been learned and how God is working in the marriages.

afterward
— Do a brief bible study discussion of "Loving By Faith" (Chapter 14, pages 166-167)

— Read "Become Accountable" (Chapter 14, pages 171 and 172) and discuss future group alternatives.

— Encouragement to take Marriage Retreat as a couple within the next two months. Brainstorm on ways to help each other be able to get away.

— Share prayer requests and close in conversational group prayer.

References

Notes

Chapter 3
1. L.L. Legters, *The Simplicity of the Spirit-Filled Life* (Farmingdale, NY: Christian Witness Products, 1930), p.21.

Chapter 6
1. Adapted from the notebook of the Family Life Conference, (a ministry of Campus Crusade for Christ, International, p. 71. Used by permission.)

2. Lawrence J. Crabb, Jr., *The Marriage Builder* (Grand Rapids, MI: Zondervan Publishing House, 1982), pp. 50, 57.

Chapter 7
1. Tim Timmons, *One Plus One* (Washington, D.C.: Canon Press, 1974), p.7.

Chapter 8
1. Tim LaHaye, *Spirit-Controlled Temperament* (Wheaton, IL: Tyndale House Publishers, 1966), p.56.
2. Charles R. Swindoll, *Strike the Original Match* (Portland, OR: Multnomah Press, 1980), pp. 100-113.
3. The material in this section was adapted from a message by Ney Bailey, National Women's Co-ordinator for Campus Crusade for Christ, U.S.A.

Chapter 9
1. Adapted from the workbook of The Family Life Conference Notebook, (a ministry of Champus Crusade for Christ, International), p. 81.

2. John Leo, "The Revolution is Over," *Time Magazine* (April 9, 1984), p.51.
3. Dr. James Dobson, *What Wives Wish their Husbands Knew About Women* (Wheaton, IL: Tyndale House, 1975), p. 116.
4. *Ibid.*, p. 127.
5. Linda Dillow, *Creative Counterpart* (Nashville, TN: Thomas Nelson, Inc., 1977), p. 90.
6. Lawrence J. Crabb, Jr. *The Marriage Builder,* (Grand Rapids, MI: Zondervan Publishing House, 1982), p. 91.

Notes

Chapter 10
1. Bruce Cook, *Faith Planning* (Wheaton, IL: Victor Books, 1983), pp. 14-17.
2. Kent Hutcheson, from a message entitled "Dreaming God's Dreams."
3. Terry Fullam in "The View From Above," *Leadership Magazine* (Winter 1984), p. 17.
4. The Leadership Dynamics Seminar Notebook, pp. 34,35. Used by permission.
5. David P. Campbell, *If you don't know where you're going, you'll probably end up somewhere else* (Niles, IL: Argus Communications, 1974), p. 16.
6. Alan Lakein, *How to Get Control of Your Time and Life* (New York, NY: New American Library, 1974), p. 25.

Chapter 11
1. Dr. Charles Sell, *Achieving the Impossible: Intimate Marriage* (Portland, OR: Multnomah Press, 1982), p. 191.
2. Larry Burkett, *How to Manage Your Money* (Chicago, IL: Moody Press, 1982), p. 7
3. Larry Burkett, *What Husbands Wish Their Wives Knew About Money* (Wheaton, IL: Victor Books, 1977), p. 85
4. Charles R. Swindoll, *Strike the Original Match* (Portland, OR: Multnomah Press, 1980), p. 118.

Chapter 12
1. Edith Schaeffer in "The Family: Worth Keeping Together," *Focus on the Family Magazine* (April, 1984) p. 3.
2. Walter A. Henrichsen, *How to Disciple Your Children* (Wheaton, IL: Victor Books, 1981), p. 88.

3. Mike Phillips, *Building Respect, Responsibility and Spiritual Values in Your Child* (Minneapolis: Bethany House Publishers, 1981), p. 65.
4. Dr. James Dobson, *Hide or Seek* (Old Tappan, NJ: Fleming H. Revell Company, 1974), p. 96,97.
5. Phillips, *op. cit.,* pp. 14,15.

Chapter 13
1. Helmut Thielicke, "The Salt, Not the Honey, of the World," *Leadership Magazine* (Winter 1983), p.119.
2. From an interview with Rebecca Manley Pippert, *Today's Christian Woman* (July/August 1984), p. 36.
3. Adapted from an exercise written by Kent Hutcheson.
4. *Pippert, op. cit.,* p. 38.
5. Larry Burkett, *Your Finances in Changing Times* (Chicago: Moody Press, 1975), p. 134.
6. *Ibid.,* p. 150.

Chapter 14
1. Leo Habets, in a message to the directors of Campus Crusade for Christ, Europe, January 1984.
2. Adapted from Bill Bright's *How to Love by Faith: Transferable Concept Eight* (San Bernardino, CA: Campus Crusade for Christ, Inc.)
3. Adapted from the notebook of the Family Life Conference (a ministry of Campus Crusade for Christ, International), pp. 130-137. Used by permission.

A Growing Garden of Resources

Note: Books published by Here's Life Publishers may be ordered directly from:

HERE'S LIFE PUBLISHERS, INC.
P.O. Box 1576
San Bernardino, CA 92402

Chapters 1, 2 and 3

Married Life:

Crabb, Lawrence J., Jr. *The Marriage Builder.* Grand Rapids, Mich.: Zondervan Publishing House, 1982. "Describes the different kinds of oneness an enriching marriage can achieve and explains both their biblical and psychological foundations.")

Strauss, Richard. *Marriage Is for Love.* Wheaton, Ill.: Tyndale House, 1977. (Espouses that couples can enjoy a "successful home life if they learn what the Bible teaches and obey it.")

Swindoll, Charles R. *Strike the Original Match.* Portland, Oreg.: Multnomah Press, 1980. (Subtitled "Rekindling and Preserving Your Marriage Fire.")

Wheat, Ed., M.D. *Love Life for Every Married Couple.* Grand Rapids, Mich.: Zondervan Publishing House, 1980. (A guide to developing the "life-long love affair God designed for husband and wife.")

——. *How to Save Your Marriage Alone.* Grand Rapids, Mich.: Zondervan Publishing House, 1983. (Deals with topics such as "Stabilizing Your Emotions:" and "Learning to Love.")

Bibliography

Spiritual Life:

Bailey, Ney. *Faith Is Not a Feeling*. San Bernardino, Calif.: Here's Life Publishers, 1978. (A thorough biblical treatment, with much personal application for the Spirit-filled walk.)

Baxter, J. Sidlow. *Majesty: The God You Should Know*. San Bernardino, Calif.: Here's Life Publishers, 1984. (Helps readers grasp the attributes of God and know Him personally in a greater way.)

Bright, Bill. *The Holy Spirit: Key to Supernatural Living*. San Bernardino, Calif.: Here's Life Publishers, 1980. (A thorough biblical treatment, with much personal application for the Spirit-filled walk.)

——. *Handbook of Concepts for Living*. San Bernardino, Calif.: Here's Life Publishers, 1981. (Practical truths for spiritual insight and joyful living, which can be transferred easily from one person to another.)

Chapin, Alice. *Bible Promises for Supernatural Living*. San Bernardino, Calif.: Here's Life Publishers, 1982. (Topically arranged to meet everyday problems, these promises uplift and inspire, no matter how tough the situation.)

Hocking, David L. *Pleasing God*. San Bernardino, Calif.: Here's Life Publishers, 1984. (Shows how to combat culture pressures, and how a lifestyle refocused on God can lead to a new wholeness and an active witnessing Christianity.)

Lindsey, Hal. *The Liberation of Planet Earth*. Grand Rapids, Mich.: Zondervan Publishing House, 1974. (Excellent on the subject of "guilt.")

McDowell, Josh. *His Image...My Image*. San Bernardino, Calif.: Here's Life Publishers, 1984. (Biblical principles and practical applications to help a person toward an improved self-image.)

McDowell, Josh, and Larson, Bart. *Jesus: A Biblical Defense of His Deity*. San Bernardino, Calif.: Here's Life Publishers, 1983. (Captivating insight into the life and person of Jesus Christ, offering proof-positive that He was and is who He claimed to be, the Savior and Redeemer.)

Packer, J. I. *Knowing God*. Downers Grove, Ill.: Inter-Varsity Press, 1973. (Insightful and inspirational examination of the nature of God and how to know Him better.)

General:

Hansel, Tim. *When I Relax I Feel Guilty*. Elgin, Ill.: David C. Cook Publishing Co., 1979. (A delightful, biblically oriented antidote to the relaxation-is-unspiritual disease.)

Maxwell, John. *Your Attitude: Key to Success*. San Bernardino, Calif.: Here's Life Publishers, 1984. (A step-by-step plan of action to help a person change his or her outlook and develop a positive, winning attitude.)

Minrith, Frank, and Meier, Paul. *Happiness Is a Choice*. Grand Rapids, Mich.: Baker Book House, 1978. (Two Christian psychiatrists outline the symptoms, causes and cures of depression.)

Chapter 6: No-Barriers Communication

Briggs, Dorothy C. *Your Child's Self-Esteem*. Garden City, N.Y.: Doubleday and Company, Inc., 1970. (Though written for parents, this secular work offers marriage partners many insights on handling anger and "I-messages.")

Howard, J. Grant. *The Trauma of Transparency*. Portland, Oreg.: Multnomah Press, 1979. (Practical, biblical help for communicating with honest and appropriate transparency.)

Powell, John. *The Secret of Staying in Love*. Niles, Ill.: Argus Communications, 1974. (Shows how communication thrives in a relationship committed to open expression.)

Small, Dwight H. *After You've Said I Do*. Old Tappan, N.J.: Fleming H. Revell, 1968. (An insightful book covering broad aspects and details of marital communication.)

Wright, H. Norman. *Communication: Key to Your Marriage*. Ventura, Calif.: Regal Books, 1974. (Contains two helpful chapters on anger.)

——. *More Communication Keys to Your Marriage*. Ventura, Calif.: Regal Books, 1983. (Includes topics such as "Communicating the Real You" and "Limiting Communication Potential.")

Chapter 7: Spiritual Oneness

Spiritual Oneness:

Crabb, Lawrence J., Jr. *The Marriage Builder*. Grand Rapids, Mich.: Zondervan Publishing House, 1982. (See especially the chapter, "Spirit Oneness: Who meets my needs?")

LaHaye, Tim. *Spirit-Controlled Family Living*. Old Tappan, N.J.: Fleming H. Revell Company, 1978. (Emphasizes the ministry of the Holy Spirit in the Christian's home life.)

Meredith, Don. *Becoming One*. Nashville, Tenn.: Thomas Nelson, Inc., 1979. (Excellent on defining spiritual oneness as a "faith marriage.")

Timmons, Tim. *One Plus One*. Washington, D.C.: Canon Press, 1974. (Delineates the biblical principles of "leaving, cleaving and one flesh.")

Bibliography

Quiet Time and Devotional Aids:

Bright, Bill. *Promises: A Daily Guide to Supernatural Living*. San Bernardino, Calif.: Here's Life Publishers, 1983. (365 daily devotionals that focus on tapping the power of Spirit-filled living.)

Bright, Vonette. *Vonette Bright's Prayer & Praise Diary*. San Bernardino, Calif.: Here's Life Publishers, 1981. (A plan for developing a more consistent and effective prayer life, arranged so that requests are remembered on a chosen day of each week.)

Brown, Joan Winmill, and Brown, Bill. *Together Each Day: Daily Devotions for Husband and Wives*. Old Tappan, N.J.: Fleming H. Revell, 1980. (Daily portions not too meaty or complex for the couple just starting to meet with God together.)

Chapin, Alice. *Bible Promises for Supernatural Living*. San Bernardino, Calif.: Here's Life Publishers, 1982. (Excellent aid to praising the Lord together.)

Foster, Richard J. *Celebration of Discipline*. San Francisco, Calif.: Harper and Row, Publishers, 1978. (A modern, challenging approach to the traditional disciplines of the Christian life, such as meditation, prayer, study and solitude.)

Green, Ken. *Personal Time Notebook*. San Bernardino, Calif.: Here's Life Publishers, 1983. (A helpful guide to developing meaningful quiet times.)

Jensen, Irving. *Do-It-Yourself Bible Studies*. San Bernardino, Calif.: Here's Life Publishers, 1983. (Inductive Bible studies.)

Purnell, Dick. *The 31-Day Experiment (Knowing God)*. San Bernardino, Calif.: Here's Life Publishers, 1984. (Anyone who wants to develop a meaningful, consistent daily time with God can approach it on a one-month trial basis.)

——. *Faith: 31-Day Experiment*. San Bernardino, Calif.: Here's Life Publishers, 1985.

Spiritual Gifts:

Flynn, Leslie B. *19 Gifts of the Spirit*. Wheaton, Ill.: Victor Books, 1974. (Subtitled "Which do you have? Are you using them?")

Yohn, Rick. *Discover Your Spiritual Gift and Use It*. Wheaton, Ill.: Tyndale House Publishers, 1974. (Well-reasoned encouragement to do just what the title says.)

Chapter 8: Understanding Each Other

Christenson, Larry and Nordis. *The Christian Couple*. Minneapolis: Bethany Fellowship, 1977. (Contains a thorough, biblical treatment of "headship" and "submission.")

Dillow, Linda. *Creative Counterpart*. Nashville, Tenn.: Thomas Nelson, Inc., 1977. (For wives; includes ideas on being husband's "greatest fan.")

Dobson, Dr. James. *What Wives Wish Their Husbands Knew about Women*. Wheaton, Ill.: Tyndale House Publishers, 1975. (For husbands; a lively discussion of the greatest sources of depression among women.)

————. *Straight Talk to Men and Their Wives*. Waco, Tex.: Word Books, 1980. (A bold redefinition of what it means to be a man, in many spheres of life.)

LaHaye, Tim. *Spirit-Controlled Temperament*. Wheaton, Ill.: Tyndale House Publishers, 1966. (A detailed look at the four basic temperaments, with emphasis on the Spirit's transforming power.)

————. *Transformed Temperaments*. Wheaton, Ill.: Tyndale House Publishers, 1971. (A study of four biblical characters who represent the four temperaments.

————. *The LaHaye Temperament Analysis*. P.O. Box 1600, San Diego, CA 92116. (For those who feel the need for greater self-knowledge. Based on a computerized text, you will receive a 15-page personalized booklet describing your strengths and weaknesses in several areas of life. Test booklets can be ordered for $24.95 each, as of this writing.)

Sell, Dr. Charles. *Achieving the Impossible: Intimate Marriage*. Portland, Oreg.: Multnomah Press, 1982. (Note especially chapter 13, which gives a balanced answer to the question, "Can we role into a happy marriage?")

Tournier, Paul. *To Understand Each Other*. Richmond, Va.: John Knox Press, 1967. (Perceptively written by a Swiss Christian physician on ways to achieve deeper understanding in marriage.)

Chapter 9: Sexual Intimacy

(For answers to specific questions concerning sexual intimacy, take either Wheat's or LaHaye's book on your marriage retreat.)

Dillow, Joseph C. *Solomon on Sex.* Nashville, Tenn.: Thomas Nelson, Inc., 1977. (A verse-by-verse commentary on the Song of Solomon, with practical application of the Scriptures to sexual love.)

Dobson, Dr. James. *What Wives Wish Their Husbands Knew About Women.* Wheaton, Ill.: Tyndale House Publishers, 1975. (Assists husbands in developing a climate of intimacy for their wives.)

LaHaye, Tim and Beverly. *The Act of Marriage.* Grand Rapids, Mich.: Zondervan Publishing House, 1976. (A practical, thorough handbook on sexual love for Christian couples.)

Sell, Dr. Charles. *Achieving The Impossible: Intimate Marriage.* Portland, Oreg.: Multnomah Press, 1982. (Includes two chapters on the biblical purpose of sex in marriage.)

Wheat, Ed, M.D., and Gaye. *Intended for Pleasure.* Old Tappan, N.J.: Fleming H. Revell Company, 1977. (A Christian physician presents medically helpful material from a godly perspective.)

Chapter 10: Living Out Priorities

Cook, Bruce. *Faith Planning.* Wheaton, Ill.: Victor Books, 1983. (Motivates toward planning with a vision of what God wants to do in our lives.)

Douglass, Stephen B. *Managing Yourself.* San Bernardino, Calif.: Here's Life Publishers, 1978. (Practical help for Christians in personal planning, time scheduling and self-control.)

Douglass, Stephen B., and Roddy, Lee. *Making the Most of Your Mind.* San Bernardino, Calif.: Here's Life Publishers, 1983. ("How to use your mind to tap into the infinite wisdom and power of God"—Josh McDowell.)

Lakein, Alan. *How to Get Control Of Your Time and Life.* New York: New American Library, 1973. (A highly readable secular text on time management.)

Ortlund, Anne. *Disciplines of the Beautiful Woman.* Waco, Tex.: Word Books, 1977. (Notice chapter 2, "Reshaping Your Life to Three Priorities.")

Yohn, Rick. *Finding Time.* Waco, Tex.: Word Books, 1984. (A practical biblical approach to management of family life. Includes a chapter on setting goals.)

Bibliography

Chapter 11: Finances

Burkett, Larry. *How to Manage Your Money*. Chicago, Ill.: Moody Press, 1982. (A workbook study of God's principles for money management: how to make it, spend it, save it, invest it and share it.)

——. *What Husbands Wish Their Wives Knew About Money*. Wheaton, Ill.: Victor Books, 1977. (Part 1 describes the changing economy as viewed through God's Word. Part 2 deals with handling money.)

——. *The Financial Planning Workbook*. Chicago, Ill.: Moody Press, 1982. (A family budgeting guide designed to bring your finances under God's control.)

Fooshee, George and Marjean. *You Can Beat the Money Squeeze*. Old Tappan, N.J.: Fleming H. Revell Company, 1980. (Points out trouble areas in budgeting, scriptural principles on money management and answers to many questions about investments.)

——. *You Can Be Financially Free*. Old Tappan, N.J.: Fleming H. Revell, 1976. (More practical advice for handling your family finances. Includes guidelines for budgeting, escaping the debt trap, and evaluating the value of a working mother.)

McLean, Gordon. *Let God Manage Your Money*. Grand Rapids, Mich.: The Zondervan Corporation, 1972. (Practical counsel on debt, buying a house or car, insurance and investing.)

Taylor, Jack. *God's Miraculous Plan of Economy*. Nashville, Tenn. Broadman Press, 1975. (The best volume for understanding Christians' responsibilities in handling money. Foundational for having a truly biblical approach to finances.)

Chapter 12: Childraising

Parenting:

Highlander, Don H. *Positive Parenting*. Waco, Tex.: Word Books, 1980. (Helps parents inventory their own parenting styles; aids in cultivating an "encouraging parenting style.")

Owen, Pat Hershey. *The Idea Book for Mothers*. Wheaton, Ill.: Tyndale House Publishers, 1981. (Includes chapters on molding dreams into realities, setting faith goals and living the Word.)

Love:

Biggs, Dorothy C. *Your Child's Self-Esteem*. Garden City, N.Y.: Doubleday and Company, 1970. (A secular book with insights into understanding yourself as a parent and your children at different stages.)

Campbell, Dr. Ross. *How to Really Love Your Child*. Wheaton, Ill.: Victor Books, 1977. (How to love your children in ways that *they* will perceive as loving.)

——. *How to Really Love Your Teenager*. Wheaton, Ill.: Victor Books, 1982. (A must for parents of teens.)

Dobson, Dr. James. *Hide or Seek*. Old Tappan, N.J.: Fleming H. Revell Company, 1979. (Building self-esteem in children.)

Discipline and Training:

Bustanoby, Andre. *Everything You Need to Know About College*. San Bernardino, Calif.: Here's Life Publishers, 1983. (A reference book for parents, pastors and youth workers who are called on to assist students considering college—and for the students themselves.)

Dobson, Dr. Fitzhugh. *How to Parent*. New York: New American Library, 1970. (A secular book. The comments on spanking are best ignored; otherwise, an immensely helpful text on child training. Contains a large bibliography of books for parents and children.)

Highlander, Don H. *Positive Parenting*. Waco, Tex.: Word Books, 1980. (Offers step-by-step guidelines for teaching responsibility and disciplining "with love and authority.")

Moore, Raymond and Dorothy. *Home Grown Kids*. Waco, Tex.: Word Books, 1981. (Subtitled "A Practical Handbook for Teaching Your Children at Home." Treats characteristics and educational guidelines for children, ages pre-birth through nine years. Filled with useful information, whether or not you are contemplating home schooling.)

Narramore, Dr. Bruce. *Help! I'm a Parent*. Grand Rapids, Mich.: Zondervan Publishing House, 1972. Explains reasons why children misbehave; offers solutions tailored to different situations.)

Swindoll, Charles R. *Your and Your Child*. Nashville, Tenn.: Thomas Nelson, Inc., 1977. (Understanding your children and raising them according to their personalities and God's principles.)

Bibliography

Temple, Dr. Joe. *Know Your Child*. Grand Rapids, Mich.: Baker Book House, 1974. (Based on scriptural directives, emphasizes ways to train each child in the direction of his own God-given abilities.)

Spiritual Guidance:

Beamer, Charles. *Joshua Wiggins and the King's Kids*. Minneapolis: Bethany House Publishers, 1981. (A series of continuing adventure stories broken into short chapters for daily devotions, each followed by related Scripture and discussion questions.)

Beers, V. Gilbert, and Beers, Ron. *Bible Stories to Live By*. San Bernardino, Calif.: Here's Life Publishers, 1983. (Written for elementary children, with Think, Learn and Do sections to help a child apply the character values that are taught. Beautifully illustrated by Dutch artist Reint De Jonge.)

——. *Walking With Jesus*. San Bernardino, Calif.: Here's Life Publishers, 1984. (Stories that point out character traits of Jesus and that teach a child how to be more like Him. Watercolor illustrations: Reint De Jonge.)

Chapin, Alice. *Building Your Child's Faith*. San Bernardino, Calif.: Here's Life Publishers, Inc., 1983. (Includes chapters on developing creative family worship and leading a child to Christ. Contains a list of fifteen months of nightly Bible readings, arranged topically.)

Henrichsen, Walter A. *How to Disciple Your Children*. Wheaton, Ill.: Victor Books, 1981. (Full of goodies! Note chapter 12, "Setting Family Goals.")

Jahsmann, Allan H., and Simon, Martin P. *Little Visits With God*. St. Louis: Concordia Publishing House, 1957. (Devotions for families with small children.)

McDowell, Josh, ed., and Stewart, Don, author. *Family Handbook of Christian Knowledge series*. San Bernardino, Calif.: Here's Life Publishers. (*The Bible*, 1983; *Creation*, 1984; *The People, The Church, Future Things*, available later.) (Richly illustrated treasure of comprehensive biblical knowledge for the entire family to explore together.)

Mow, Anna B. *Your Child From Birth to Rebirth*. Grand Rapids, Mich.: Zondervan Publishing House, 1963. (Developing Christian character in children.)

Bibliography

Schoolland, Marian M. *Leading Little Ones to God*. Grand Rapids, Mich.: Wm. B. Eerdmans Publishing Company, 1981. (A child's book of doctrinal Bible teachings, in daily devotional form.)

Shibley, David and Naomi. *Special Times With God*. Nashville, Tenn.: Thomas Nelson Publishers, 1981. (Basic Bible teachings in short devotional form for small children.)

Skold, Betty W. *Lord, I Have a Question*. Minneapolis: Augsburg Publishing House, 1979. (Story devotions for preteen girls. Several titles available, also for boys, in Augsburg's "Young Readers" series.)

Taylor, Kenneth N. *The Bible in Pictures for Little Eyes*. Chicago: Moody Press, 1956. (For very young children.)

——. *Stories for the Children's Hour*. Chicago: Moody Press, 1968. (Devotions giving insight into the behavior Jesus wants, with questions and answers after each chapter.)

Vos, Catherine F. *The Child's Story Bible*. Grand Rapids, Mich. William B. Eerdmans, 1935. (Our favorite Bible story book for school-age children.)

Family Activities:

Bock, Lois, and Working, Miji. *Happiness is a Family Night at Home*. Old Tappan, N.J.: Fleming H. Revell Company, 1975. (Subtitled "Learning more about God and each other.")

Gaither, Gloria, and Dobson, Shirley. *Let's Make a Memory*. Waco, Tex.: Word Books, 1983. (Two prominent Christian women offer ideas for making special family times memorable.)

Rickerson, Wayne. *Christian Family Activities*. Cincinnatti: Standard Publishing, 1982. (Available for preschoolers, children or teens. We have used these Bible-based activities and discussions successfully with our own family.)

Riddell, Carole, and Wallingford, Kay. *Helpful Hints for Fun-Filled Parenting*. Nashville, Tenn.: Thomas Nelson Publishers, 1984. (Includes over 750 "Why-didn't-I-think-of-that?" tips, many of which can be adapted for family fun times.)

Magazines:

Dads Only/Moms and Dads. P.O. Box 340, Julian, CA 92036. (A monthly newsletter filled with creative ideas to aid parents in building Christ-centered homes.)

Family Life Today. P.O. Box 1971, Marion, OH 43305. (A "survival kit" for Christian families. Many helpful articles on sensitive issues, plus daily devotional readings with discussion questions.)

Focus on the Family. Published by Focus on the Family, P.O. Box 500, Arcadia, CA 91006. (An extension of Dr. James Dobson's ministry. Subscription is provided at no charge.)

Chapter 13: Fruit That Won't Rot

Books to Loan the Seeker or Skeptic:

Lewis, C.S. *Mere Christianity*. New York: MacMillan Publishing Company, 1960. (A classic volume, spelling out for the thoughtful skeptic the essentials of Christianity in a compelling style.)

McDowell, Josh. *Evidence That Demands a Verdict*. San Bernardino, Calif.: Here's Life Publishers, 1972. This highly acclaimed best seller is a thorough defense of Christian belief. Well-grounded answers for the most critical skeptic willing to honestly weigh the evidence.)

———. *More Than a Carpenter*. Wheaton, Ill.: Tyndale House Publishers, 1977. (An easy-to-read book for people who are skeptical about Jesus' deity, His resurrection and His claims on their lives, with chapters like "Lord, Liar or Lunatic?" and "Will the Real Messiah Please Stand Up?")

Montgomery, John Warwick. *History and Christianity*. San Bernardino, Calif.: Here's Life Publishers, 1983. (Professor Montgomery's cogent, well-reasoned defense of the historical reliability of the New Testament documents and their relevance today.)

Stewart, Don. *You Be the Judge*. San Bernardino, Calif.: Here's Life Publishers, 1983. (Offers the reader a chance to judge for himself the evidence concerning Christ's deity and resurrection, the reliability of the Bible, and fulfilled prophecy.)

Personal Evangelism:

Aldrich, Joseph C. *Life-Style Evangelism*. Portland, Oreg.: Multnomah Press, 1981. (In this provocative volume, the author challenges many widely held views and describes what evangelism should be. Includes many practical ideas for outreach through your testimony, discovery groups, and with neighbors.)

Bright, Bill. *A Handbook of Concepts for Living*. San Bernardino, Calif.: Here's Life Publishers, 1981. (A practical, easy-to-follow guide for Christian growth. Includes chapters on "How to Introduce Others to Christ" and "How to Witness in the Spirit.")

Ford, Leighton. *Good News Is for Sharing*. Elgin, Ill.: David C. Cook Publishing Company, 1977. (Encourages practical involvement in evangelism. Includes helpful chapters on "Why do I get nervous about sharing my faith?" and "How do I find out the point where people are hurting?")

Little, Paul E. *How to Give Away Your Faith*. Chicago, Ill.: Inter-Varsity Press, 1966. (The classic textbook on instruction for doing personal evangelism, including answers to the seven basic objections raised by non-Christians.)

Leadership Resources:

Bailey, Ney, and Stoop, David. *Faith is Not a Feeling Growth Guide*. San Bernardino, Calif.: Here's Life Publishers, 1983. (Designed to accompany the sourcebook for understanding God's total trustworthiness. A warm-hearted account of what it means to walk with God by faith. Video tape available to deepen interaction.)

Campus Crusade for Christ. *The Discipleship Series*. San Bernardino, Calif.: Here's Life Publishers, 1983. (Unique studies for (1) Discovery groups, (2) Growth groups and (3) teaching others to lead the same. Each level has a book for group members and a thorough Leader's Guide to help you disciple people in an optimum environment.)

Hicks, Robert, and Bewes, Richard. *Understanding Bible Truth*. San Bernardino, Calif.: Here's Life Publishers, 1981. (A nine-booklet series covering a whole range of Bible teaching. Helps clarify essential facts and gives open-ended questions for Discovery, Growth, and Bible study groups.)

Bibliography

The Navigators. *How to Lead Small Group Bible Studies.* Colorado Springs, Colo.: Navpress, 1982. (Contains everything you need to know to start and continue a group successfully. Focuses on how to be a good moderator and guide.)

Peddicord, Clark. *Life of Christ Growth Guide.* San Bernardino, Calif.: Here's Life Publishers, 1984. (A two-book series of guided studies and rich background material, exploring Christ's life through the eyes of Mark. Excellent for Growth groups and Bible study groups.)

Chapter 14: Subdue Weekly Weeds

(Books that contain questions in each chapter as resources for ongoing Talk Times.)

Arp, Claudia and Dave. *Ten Dates for Mates.* Nashville, Tenn. Thomas Nelson Publishers, 1983.

Barber, Cyril and Aldyth. *Your Marriage Has Real Possibilities.* Grand Rapids, Mich.: Kregel Publications, 1981.

————. *You Can Have a Happy Marriage.* Grand Rapids, Mich.: Kregel Publications, 1984.

The Navigators. *Husbands and Wives.* Colorado Springs, Colo. Navpress, 1980.

Rickerson, Wayne. *We Never Have Time For Just Us.* Ventura, Calif.: Regal Books, 1982.

Roberts, Wes and Judy, and Wright, H. Norman. *After You Say I Do.* Eugene, Oreg.: Harvest House Publishers, 1979.

Wright, H. Norman. *The Pillars of Marriage.* Ventura, Calif.: Regal Books, 1979.

TAPES FOR STIMULATING MARRIAGE GROWTH

The following cassette tape albums are recommended for enriching your marriage and stimulating communication on vital issues.

For prices and mail orders, write to:

Foundations for Family Living Tapes
P.O. Box 55330
Little Rock, AR 72225

Oneness: God's Design for Marriage (four tapes). This series can help you consistently appreciate your mate, experience freedom in your marriage role, reconcile frictions while they are small, and much more. You also can use it as a six- to eight-week guide to stimulate thought and discussion in Sunday School classes, home Bible studies and studies with couples.

Communication and Sex in Marriage (two tapes). Through this thought-provoking series, you can learn to experience the joy of heart-to-heart communication, achieve sexual fulfillment, deal with conflict constructively and add romance to your relationship.

Bibliography

Love Life, by Ed Wheat, M.D. (two tapes). Learn how to fall in love with your mate and stay in love, how to restore love to any marriage (even if it seems hopeless), and how to add more love to an already good marriage.

Sex Techniques and Sex Problems in Marriage, by Ed Wheat, M.D. (two tapes). Dr. Wheat sensitively and reverently answers questions about sexual fulfillment and dysfunction.

Dad, the Family Shepherd (three tapes). This package provides forthright help and encouragement for leading the family in this difficult age of pressure and stress. The messages address the husband's role as shepherd, manager and minister.

Partners for Life (three tapes). A unique interview with Bill Bright, president and founder of Campus Crusade for Christ, and his wife, Vonette, who share personal insights into the success of their marriage of more than thirty-three years. (Dennis Rainey, national director of the Family Ministry, and his wife, Barbara, interview the Brights.)

Preparing for Oneness (three tapes). This timely biblical instruction has helped many couples begin their marriages on the right foundation and has enhanced their relationships. It makes an ideal gift for engaged couples.

Notes

Notes

Notes

Notes

Notes

Notes

Notes

Notes

Notes

Notes

Notes

Notes

Notes

Notes